THE
ECONOMICS
OF THE
CONSTRUCTION
INDUSTRY

GERALD FINKEL

M.E. Sharpe
Armonk, New York
London, England

Copyright © 1997 by Gerald Finkel

All rights reserved. No part of this book may be reproduced in any form
without written permission from the publisher, M. E. Sharpe, Inc.,
80 Business Park Drive, Armonk, New York 10504.

Library of Congress Cataloging-in-Publication Data

Finkel, Gerald.
The economics of the construction industry /
Gerald Finkel.
p.   cm.
Includes bibliographical references and index.
ISBN 1-56324-986-3 (hc : alk. paper). —
ISBN 1-56324-987-1 (pbk. : alk. paper)
1. Construction industry—United States.
I. Title.
HD9715.U52F52   1997
338.4'769'00973—dc20
96–44648
CIP

Printed in the United States of America

The paper used in this publication meets the minimum requirements of the
American National Standard for Information Sciences—
Permanence of Paper for Printed Library Materials,
ANSI Z 39.48-1984.

EB (c)   10   9   8   7   6   5   4   3   2   1
EB (p)   10   9   8   7   6   5   4   3   2   1

To Helen, Margot, and Suzanne,
for their love and understanding

CONTENTS

LIST OF TABLES AND FIGURES

Tables

Figures

ACKNOWLEDGMENTS

Many of the ideas and concepts for this book were developed on two levels. In an academic setting, courses on the construction industry that I have taught at the Harry Van Arsdale Jr. School for Labor Studies provided an incentive and purpose for my research. In addition, discussions with the late Professor David M. Gordon of the Graduate Faculty of the New School for Social Research helped to frame issues surrounding productivity and workplace relations. I should also thank Professor Lois Gray from the Cornell University School of Industrial Relations for her kind suggestions and encouragement as well as Francine Meccio from Cornell's Institute for Women and Work.

In a practical sense, I would also like to acknowledge my day-to-day experiences in the New York City electrical construction industry as an important influence on this work. Building trades workers, employers, union representatives, and construction managers have provided me with invaluable insights into construction activity. I am also grateful to Rosemarie Fogarty and her co-workers at the U.S. Department of Commerce in Manhattan for their prompt responses to requests for construction industry data.

Finally, my thanks to the staff at M.E. Sharpe; in particular, Stephen Dalphin for his consideration, Esther Clark for her organizing skills, and Eileen Gaffney for a careful review of my finished product.

THE
ECONOMICS
OF THE
CONSTRUCTION
INDUSTRY

INTRODUCTION

The American construction industry is a vibrant and dynamic segment of the overall economy. It is annually responsible for nearly 4 percent of the nation's gross domestic product (GDP). In 1996 construction provided jobs for more than 5 million people and nearly 1.5 million support jobs in related fields. Despite this key role in the overall economy, there have been few major economic works that have focused on this important domestic industry. Construction economics remains relegated to engineering and estimating, while labor relations are often seen as an offshoot of the industrial collective bargaining experience.

Seminal works, such as those about the Chicago building trades by Stephen Sobotka (1953) or Lawrence Kahn's comparative study of the San Francisco and Los Angeles building industries (1978), focused on localized markets. Path-breaking texts, such as William Haber and Harold Levinson's (1956), were narrowly defined toward union market mechanisms. More recent books by Daniel Q. Mills (1972b) and Peter Cassimatis (1969) and studies by Steven Allen (1985, 1986, 1994) have substantially contributed to a greater appreciation of the economic impact of this industrial sector.

Mills's *Industrial Relations and Manpower in Construction* carefully developed an analysis of the many economic characteristics within the construction markets. While such a work enhances our overall understanding of the construction market, the topics and issues sorely need to be updated. Cassimatis's brief but enlightening research project confronts much of what historically mystifies analysts of the building industry. Size and output seem to have a cloudy statistical relationship, while the small-firm nature of a large portion of the industry defies the trends that typically appear within other industrial sectors.

Why is research and development so lacking in the hands-on segment of construction? What role do unions play in retarding or advancing technological development? Why have consolidation and mergers failed to restructure the industry to a larger extent? Certainly Cassimatis's production functions and his concentration on input/output functions were important analytical additions to the existing body of literature. Although Cassimatis did his work over thirty years ago, many of his observations hold true in present circumstances.

This text aims to advance our knowledge of construction markets by providing an introductory-level view of the issues that surround the building industry. The research will draw together the many facets of the building industry and develop a general understanding of its intricacies. It is written in a fashion that lends itself to use by those directly involved in the industry as well as those who might simply be curious about the world of concrete, pipe, and steel.

The industry itself is fragmented and diverse. Mom-and-Pop shops operate alongside of multibillion-dollar construction conglomerates. Powerful trade unions are forced to deal with the realities of the highly competitive aspects of the building industry, such as alterations and single-family dwellings. Technologically, construction is constrained by its own peculiar nature. Highly durable products are custom designed and installed through a multitude of manual operations. Competitive requirements relegate field research and development to the back burner, while job competition and cyclical employment make nonsupervisory personnel leery of productivity enhancements.

This study is divided into fifteen chapters. The first chapter examines the historical development of building activity because the modern-day industry of high-rise and low-rise structures is firmly rooted in centuries-old building practices. The issues of illumination, ventilation, strength, and support have troubled every generation since time immemorial. Yet, as successive societies have grappled with these problems, their solutions have reflected the social and economic conditions of the time.

The modern era is clearly no exception. Nineteenth-century skyscrapers appear when demographic shifts lead to increasing land prices. In a scant one hundred years, urban centers came to be defined by their skylines, while suburban sprawls were soon dotted by massive factory settings and surrounding bedroom communities. Those developments are reviewed through the changes of building materials, technology, and the workplace itself.

Chapter 2 provides a brief introduction to a series of competing economic theoretical explanations of the workings of the construction industry. The writings of Adam Smith, Karl Marx, and John Maynard Keynes are uniquely applied to the modern era of private and public construction. Since no conclusion is drawn as to the merits of these competing views, the reader is left with three alternative explanations from which to choose. As a primer on the economics of the industry, the arguments developed over the next several pages need to be rooted in past and current economic thought. Market instability, cyclically high unemployment, and uneven investment patterns seem wanting of a better explanation than the often cited "it's the nature of construction."

The third chapter begins to examine the specifics of the modern American construction industry. In the United States, the building industry moved rapidly from the era of artisans and independent journeypersons to the full-blown development of market-based construction. The preeminence of contract construction was very apparent by the first quarter of the twentieth century. The buyers and sellers of construction skills and abilities were soon positioned as competitive units of capital or labor vying in a world of limited resources. Such conditions were typical of capitalistic production processes throughout the economy, and the building industry was quickly consumed in this mode of production. Today, the multibillion-dollar industry is parceled out among government-financed projects, private developers, corporate needs, and structures that are mixed in use. The market distinctions and barriers often seem as loosely structured and ill-defined as the construction process itself appears to the untrained observer.

Yet, for all the static and conservative elements that abound, there have been noticeable degrees of change and discernible trends. Chapter 4 examines some of these trends. One of the key measures of construction industry performance is the industry's contribution to the nation's GDP. The chapter begins with a review of this performance, using GDP as a point of departure to highlight specific industry-related issues. For example, the forms of employment were altered as employers became increasingly specialized. Following the logic of technological developments, workers began seeking employment in narrowly defined trades as plumbers, steamfitters, electricians, and elevator constructors. Workers wrestled with job descriptions and their requirements as construction entered a brave new world regulated by the clock and guided by the developer's demand schedule. The ultimate response from the working class was the formation of skilled-trade unions.

Modern construction unions, while owing a debt to the nascent craft organizations of the nineteenth century, have developed into extraordinarily complex institutions. With memberships in the millions of workers, these trade unions are comprised of thousands of local jurisdictions, each with its own unique set of market requirements and contractual relationships. Union workers have established a considerable presence on medium-sized to large commercial, government, and residential projects. Nonunion contractors and workers continue to perform the bulk of the work on small-scale jobs and one-family residential developments, however, and there is increasing evidence that the market share for nonunion contractors has been expanding since the 1980s. Herbert Northrup has estimated that open-shop construction firms could account for as much as 80 percent of the dollar output produced by building firms (Northrup 1993, p. 470).

The trends in unionism are only a piece of the entire picture. Changes in labor-force participation by female and minority workers have begun to reshape the image of the rough-hewn male hard-hat. Following the passage of the 1960s civil rights legislation, affirmative action and government set-asides were created to increase the opportunities for minority and female contractors and workers. The efficacy and impact of some of these programs are the subject of a brief examination.

Structural change caused by mergers and acquisitions is more frequent among design and engineering firms. However, the nonoccurrence of capital concentration is itself important for what it says about change in the industry. When this does take place within construction installation firms, it presents a diversion from the historic progression of apprentice to journeyperson to contractor that typified an earlier period. It is the discussion of these trends that marks the fourth chapter.

Although change in this industry is mediated by the internal dynamics of workers, employers, and the ultimate users of the finished product, measurement of performance in the industry has always been somewhat tenuous. Chapter 5 discusses the weighty problem of construction measures. A diverse supply of statistical data and indices raises questions in the analysis of an enormous collection of construction products.

There are several reliable sources for information on current and past construction firm performances. *Construction Review* (U.S. Department of Commerce) is the most focused of all and provides extensive data on the value of new construction put in place. *County Business Patterns* (Bureau of the Census) presents detailed survey characteristics of firm sizes and employment by county. Other sources are the *Survey of Current Business* (U.S. Department of Commerce) and the Bureau of Labor Statistics (U.S. Department of Labor). The variation in sources and the differences in research focus present a challenge in the use of compatible data.

Thus, explaining the variation in output levels in the construction industry is by no means an easy task. Chapter 6 centers on construction investment and growth. The dramatic cyclical movements in outputs and employment are considered in light of the sources for construction spending and the basis for this demand. Durability, inventory, and economic expansion are important variables that affect the rate and level of construction investment. In particular the housing industry serves as a model of the investment process and its wider economic implications. The chapter also looks at the role of the investment accelerator in construction investment.

Chapter 7 focuses on the key role of the public sector, as both a buyer of construction services and a regulator of industry practices. The tremendous impact of government at the federal, state, and local levels is examined from political and economic angles. This includes a discussion of the legal framework pertaining to unions as institutions and an introduction to the role of the state in wage determination. A number of recent court and board decisions serve to explain the wide range of current government involvement in industry and market activities.

Statistical questions, investment decisions, and past and current trends are still peripheral to the heart of any industrial sector. Real economic thrust is found in the levels and rates of change of an industry's productivity. Chapter 8 reviews a number of topics surrounding the productivity issue. What improvements have taken place to further productivity? Or is productivity in construction declining, and by what measures is such a conclusion reached? The chapter introduces the relationship between output and labor-intense field operations. It then looks at prefabrication and the general failure of the industry to create economies of scale. The discussion ends with a restatement of the deflator problem, which leads into the specific studies on productivity in the next section.

Productivity is reviewed in the ninth chapter with an eye toward the role unions play in job site output. This long-standing debate is reviewed through a series of case studies that focus on the union/nonunion productivity issue. The chapter combines a historical survey with a look at more recent analytical perspectives. This is accomplished by updating an older measurement series on industry productivity for the purpose of evaluating trends in construction worker output. The research gives a practical insight into the problem of real output change while furnishing a consistent time series of hourly output. Reasonable measures and proxies exist, and the reader will be introduced to data and recent research on construction productivity.

Standing behind the productivity issue are a host of microeconomic considerations. Chapter 10 serves as an introduction to this segment of the analysis by presenting a discussion of competition in the construction industry. The ways in which employers compete with other employers and workers compete with other workers underscore the role of the market forces in this industry.

Included in chapter 10 is a section devoted to what can simply be called workplace management and workplace control. What structures are created to facilitate a stable and smoothly run workplace? The section highlights the importance of hands-on skills and the differences between manufacturing and construction managerial options as viewed from mainstream, institutional, and radical economic positions.

Almost at the bottom of the list in chapter 11 is the review of the determinants of construction workers' wages. The union/nonunion differential is a well-documented fact varying over time by trade and locale. Traditional assumptions about influences on wages are examined by applying orthodox economic arguments about sources of wage change. These are contrasted with institutional positions along with some recent less traditional approaches to the wage question. Workers are passive participants who can at best withhold their services as a last resort. In many ways, this ignores the human side of the trade union movement, which has always relied on the social bonds between workers for its basic strengths.

Chapters 12 and 13 look at the contrasting views of the distinct labor markets in the industry. The discussions focus on differences in the union and nonunion sectors. Chapter 12 focuses primarily on the union as an institutional participant in the construction industry. The origins of the building trade unions are traced from their historical roots through their twentieth-century development. The overview is brought up to date with an investigation of the current debates on the role of the modern trade union.

Chapter 13, on industry training, discusses apprenticeships, government intervention, and productivity. While this can provide only a cursory look into market operations, it is evident that the growing open-shop movement has become a type of institution on its own. The call for expanded training programs and contractor funding at a recent Associated Builders and Contractors convention marked a change in this organization's focus and underscored the overall importance of formal skill development.

Chapter 14 reviews the critical issue of safety in the workplace. Public policies with respect to occupational safety and health, compensation, and toxic substances have been of considerable concern. Yet safety can appear alternatively as a cost, a benefit, and a workplace right. A discussion of these aspects in the final chapter rounds out this introduction to the economics of the construction industry.

The wide range of elements found in the text are pulled together by concluding remarks in chapter 15. It includes some suggestions for future research as well as policy implications that could prove beneficial to those who earn their livelihoods from construction and those who depend on its services.

CHAPTER 1

The Historical Development of the Construction Market

There are two underlying themes that permeate the modern building industry. The first is that construction per se is technologically rooted in man's historical appropriation of nature. The second is that the present-day notion of construction as an economic sector is an outgrowth of the development of market-based construction. Both of these themes are inexorably woven into the everyday pace and rhythm of construction.

In the first respect, builders and craftspersons still confront the age-old problems posed in the aboriginal search for dwellings. Issues of ventilation, illumination, and structural support, which challenged their historical predecessors, are confronted daily by engineers, architects, and tradespersons. Cave dwellers would no more be apt to build a wintry fire in a low-domed cliff aperture than would a twentieth-century architect design a sealed office structure without air-conditioning.

The physical history of construction is one of materials and machines. The choice of materials has always been a function of use, durability, and availability. Brick and stone structures dominated colonial New England while timber homes were the western standards. The ice structures of the frozen northlands and the adobe homes of the sun-dried Southwest highlight the obvious in technique and medium.

Yet all of these materials have inherent structural limitations and therefore limited use value. Changes in technologies and materials were greatly affected by the activity in related markets (e.g., real estate and transportation). Thus the decisions on employment of scarce resources were shaped as much by technical considerations as by economic concerns.

There are several building staples that can be used to illustrate the preceding arguments. The weekend handyperson's all-purpose medium—wood—provides a good starting point. Timber, its natural fibers plentiful and accessible in so much of the world, has played a pivotal role in the development of the construction industry. Strong and durable, light and readily cut to size, wood has always been the preeminent builder's material.

As special handlers and installers of wood, carpenters trace their roots to biblical times. Wood in the form of timber, planks, and boards worked well in all phases of the building process. Ladders, supports, scaffolds, and decking could quickly be constructed from wood. For centuries, finished products of wood kept sailors afloat and landlubbers warm as wood became the defining element of construction activity.

The tensile and lateral strengths of wood are powerful indeed. Cross beams, roof beams, and header beams of lengths up to forty feet provided dependable support to buildings as high as six stories. Multistory dwellings, barns, and farmhouses dotted the eighteenth-century American landscape as testimony to the practical advantages of wooden construction.

Yet for all its sturdiness, wood also brings with it a number of limitations. Low-rise and single-family dwellings were and still are adequately supported with wood framing. It is around the seventh-story level that such structures falter. Wooden beams and joints are not capable of withstanding the rigorous stress of high-rise building. Wind, settling shifts, and overall weight create engineering disasters. The shoring up of columns and joists would create an unusually complex shelter if wood were used in a high-rise building.

Even if weight considerations were eliminated, timber costs in terms of time and material would be prohibitive. While the longevity of wood is legendary (ancient Mediterranean piers have been found intact), its exposure to the elements presents a serious maintenance issue. After all, the Colosseum in Rome and the temples of Athens endure precisely because of their nonwooden construction.

In the twentieth century a series of issues came together to inhibit the attraction to wood. Flammability is clearly a concern in densely populated urban areas, and building codes severely reduced wood's applications. Deforestation is a second issue, and has as much to do with the rising cost of scarce timber as it does with environmental shock over shrinking timberlands. The vociferous demand for raw building wood as well as for finished wooden products helped to trigger market mechanisms such as product substitution and labor-saving techniques.

A modern alternative to wood has clearly been steel. Developed out of the iron ore industry, steel is a metallic alloy compound of carbon and iron. The relatively low carbon content in steel distinguishes it from its forerunner—cast iron. Steel was found to be more malleable and lighter than cast iron, making it an almost instant "hit" among builders. It was not long after the introduction of steel to the building industry that nineteenth-century steel structures were surpassing the heights of such skyscraping marvels as the Cast Iron Building in Manhattan.

By the turn of the twentieth century, steel and commercial construction were literally welded together for the future. The steel I beam could provide enormous transverse support resulting in a reduced number of vertical supports. With office market rents based on square footage, fewer supports meant greater amounts of rentable space. The incremental costs of steel construction could readily be justified by the added revenues steel would bring. The durability, strength, and fire resistance of the metal easily made up the cost differential in installation and production. Iron ore gave rise to the ironworker, and an essentially highly skilled modern building trade was born. Riveters, erectors, and welders became permanent fixtures on the construction scene as they plied their trade on structural skeletons with seeming abandon.

In addition, steel was readily integrated into the core construction of any project. Thin steel girders were capable of supporting wide expanses of concrete flooring and the form work that went with these poured decks. Banks of elevators and the vertical steel rails upon which they ran were incorporated into the steel framework, with iron and concrete stairwells being easily connected to the internal superstructure.

While the technical factors favoring steel seem commonsensical, the cost savings were far less obvious. A convergence of diverse market activities formed a late-nineteenth-century nexus that resulted in a classic matching of supply with demand. For the barons of steel, this marked the beginnings of an unmistakable boom. For the in-house fabricators of steel products, it represented additional pressure on the unions and the workers' control of the production process. For on-site constructors, it signaled the commencement of a tidal wave of construction that has yet to subside.

The symbiotic relationship of construction with related markets is not a new story. Balloon-frame construction of single-family homes rapidly replaced tongue-and-groove framing of American homes in the mid-nineteenth century (Fitchen 1986, p. 67). Rising demand for housing in the western states was coupled with a relative lack of skilled carpentry labor. Yet, as Boorstin has noted, "such a breakthrough in home building could never have taken place without revolutionary advances in the manufacturing of nails" (Boorstin 1965, p. 150).*

In a similar vein, steel construction was reliant upon a manufacturing advancement that appeared in the form of the Bessemer (or Kelly) method. The cheapened cost of quality steel was a boon to the railroads, construction firms, and manufacturers of the time.

As a practical marketing strategy for steel producers, the advent of the high-rise building was a godsend. The consolidation and expansion of enterprise following the end of Civil War hostilities led to a wave of immigration on the coasts. The flow of immigrants to port cities such as New York City and Boston put a strain on available land resources. In short, the solution to the resulting rise in land values was to cease building out and begin building up. Such a solution necessitated a new structural form.

Steel played still another role in the development of America's late-nineteenth-century economic expansion. The rising populations of the eastern cities required an efficient transportation network that could move raw materials and finished products. It was this growing use of steel in the cities and on the rails that helped to create the framework for a national economy.

The famous meeting of the Union Pacific's and the Central Pacific's railroad construction companies at Promontory Point, Utah, in 1869 was a watershed for iron rail construction. By 1900 there were almost 200,000 miles of railroads in the United States. With the crisscrossing of the continent in iron and steel rails, the market for steel had lived up to expectations. As markets mature, new outlets are typically sought by producers. It was the building industry that offered the perfect flow in

---

* Balloon frames require the nailing of studs and cross beams made of two-by-four-inch and four-by-four-inch pieces of wood. Tongue-and-groove frames required the skilled shaping of a timber end into a tenon which fit precisely into a mortise.

demand. The investments of the steel magnates were not justified for a market confined to rail systems. It was the involvement in a much broader scope of economic activity that was the real prize (Chandler 1965, p. 77).

This same type of market integration must also be considered when reviewing the third key building material. Concrete is produced by mixing granular deposits with a cementious binder. The binder is usually in a powdered form containing a mix of elements such as silica and lime. Its natural appearance in many parts of the world helped give concrete a grand and glorious role in the history of construction. From Roman aqueducts to cathedral towers, concrete has been molded into structures of use and shelters of sanctuary. Yet the historic role of concrete changed rapidly with the fast pace of modern economic development.

Since antiquity, concrete had been used to provide durable and maintenance-free coverings for a variety of structures. It was shaped by bricks or stone, which became part of the permanent work (e.g., the aqueducts), or spread over on top of various fills to form a platform, as in the Mediterranean docks. Despite its widespread applications and relative availability on a large scale, there was little generalized commercial use of concrete. For one thing, concrete lacked tensile strength to complement its ability to cover large areas. For another, the dependence on natural cementious binders limited supply and confined the locations for production. Concrete's historic importance as a building material belied the fact that concrete work remained archaic.

Once again it is the latter part of the twentieth century that is the backdrop for the development of a modern concrete industry. The significant breakthroughs were the invention of Portland cement and the innovation of reinforced concrete. Portland cement became the artificial binder that held together the granular particles, thus overcoming the natural limitations imposed by cement deposits. Reinforced concrete was created through the combination of concrete and steel. The placement of steel rods into wet concrete helped to solve the problem of tensile strength. The hardening of cement around these invisible supports produced a powerful finished product that could sustain massive weight over wide expanses.

With a concrete industry in place, the trucking of cement became one of the integral operations in the construction industry. Concrete laborers, cement finishers, and drivers would be sought for skilled and semiskilled positions that provided tens of thousands of jobs for immigrants and native Americans alike. It did not take long before the time necessary for the pouring and hardening of the deck set the pace for any new project. By 1917 concrete technology had reached the point where Anheuser-Busch could construct the world's largest concrete building in St. Louis. At eight stories and 21.3 million cubic feet, it stood as a solid monument to the growth of construction design.

As with the other cases cited, concrete design had built-in limitations. The tensile strength of poured reinforced concrete and the weight of the finished pour required large amounts of columnar support. Unlike steel frames and decking, which could create large open commercial spaces, concrete decking needed more closely arranged under-supports. Thus the relative costs of concrete as opposed to steel made concrete more suitable for high-rise housing and low-rise commercial projects.

Because apartments are rented or sold by the number of rooms in the unit rather than by square-foot area, columns that could be integrated into wall or closet designs were not a serious drawback to prospective tenants. The concrete system of flying (reusable) plywood forms and four-by-four-inch wooden posts provided an inexpensive means of keeping floor pours on cycles as short as two days, with only one day to build forms and only one to pour.

Engineering and design advances were able to compensate for the weight issues, and by the mid-twentieth century concrete structures began to rise to extraordinary heights. Through the use of setbacks and relocation of core components such as elevators and mechanical rooms, architects and engineers found the structural strength to propel these buildings skyward. For example, in 1967 construction workers were nearing completion of the Lakepoint Tower in Chicago, a seventy-story reinforced concrete building.

Regardless of how innovative these architects and engineers may have been with their newly created building materials, high-rise construction still could not have proceeded without several additional technical breakthroughs. Practically speaking, electric power and indoor plumbing needed further advancements before skyscrapers could be used efficiently. More to the point, there could be no such skyward movements without the invention of the elevator.

Of the dazzling array of nineteenth-century construction breakthroughs, the electric-powered elevator symbolizes the confluence of industry, economy, and technology. Mechanical lifting was not new to builders or architects. Pulley systems powered by humans or animals were in existence throughout the ages. But this type of lifting was designed exclusively for materials, for the usual ropes of hemp proved far too unreliable for passengers.

The turn-of-the-nineteenth-century application of steam power and the creation of a steam-powered hydraulic lift were the first real shifts in lift construction in centuries. The use of a piston operated by a pressurized fluid improved lifting capability, but it was Elisha Otis's safety device that solved the problem of reliability. The Otis braking mechanism, which was attached to the steel rails, provided the security to overcome the inherent dangers of worn-out rope systems.

By 1857 the first steam-powered hydraulic people lift was operating in the Haughworth department store in New York City, moving people up and down through five stories. In the mid-1880s electric power replaced steam and the first commercial application of an electric-powered non-hydraulic lift appeared in the Demarest Building in New York City.

Vertical transportation had become an industry unto itself. From manufacture to installation, elevators were now big business. In the same manner that electricity gave rise to the electrician and steel to the steelworker, the elevator produced the elevator constructor. The technologies of steel, hydraulics, and electricity were being combined at the job site through a myriad of skilled workers and specialty contractors.

Development was urgent and moved ahead rapidly. High-rise construction was pointless without vertical lifts. As building heights spiraled upward, elevator technology raced alongside. The 102-story Empire State Building was constructed with elevators capable of moving people skyward at the rate of 1,200 feet per minute, while in less than 100 years from the first commercial use, elevators in the 110-story World Trade Center were climbing at a rate of 1,800 feet per minute, or nearly three floors per second.

The histories of other engineering and architectural challenges are not dissimilar to those of structural support and human mobility. Electricity, electric lights, ventilation, and environmental controls had periods of discovery, experimentation, and commercialization. The common economic path that connected these various aspects of construction is found in the basic principles of market economics. Low-cost production, product availability, and quality control are important elements to the satisfaction of market demand. The unfolding of the construction industry has been to a great extent the response to endogenous economic factors. Thus once the machinery has been set in place, the same rules that apply to overall market enterprise begin to take hold in a particular market. Competition, profitability, wage labor, and productivity are historically developed categories that need to be more fully understood in terms of the development of the construction industry.

Yet while so many of the rules of an enterprise system are applicable, these same rules are mediated by the unique characteristics of the building industry. In particular, falsework, geographic location, and hand-tool operations have helped to shape the direction and pace of the industry.

Falsework refers to the amount of temporary construction needed to build a final structure. This can consist of scaffolding, ladders, and formwork. It can be found on every job site from the Egyptian pyramids to the Battery Park City complex in New York. Not surprisingly, falsework has its own special skill requirements and engineering concerns. On the modern site, cost concerns continue to drive contractors toward efficient use of temporary work. This produces a continual search for means of integrating falsework into the final product.

The formidable task of architects and engineers is to devise structures that assist in construction and can later be integrated into the finished product. This can be as simple as the use of a roof beam for hoisting materials on a one-family house or as complex as employing future ventilating shafts as temporary worker entrances on a tunnel construction site.

Geographic location is important because it creates an almost natural barrier to outside competitors. As the construction market evolved from distinguishable local markets into a loosely connected national and regional system, competition increased among employers and workers. Yet, local construction competition necessarily takes place under the same code regulations, area standards, and building practices. Capable and established builders in one locale may find it difficult to enter markets that are a considerable distance from the company's home base.

Units of capital could be invested across several regions, but the points of production would ultimately be determined by the user's needs. Overseas competition and geographic variations are important factors in the search for location, but they are readily blunted by other market considerations. Proximity to clients, financial sources, labor pool qualities, and tax structures can often offset local higher building costs.

It is probably the character of the labor process more than any single feature that truly defines the internal dynamics of the building industry. The workplace has always been and still remains highly labor inten- sive. While the pace of the manufacturing plant is readily influenced by the speed of the assembly line and the manager's watchful eye, these controls cannot easily be adapted to the construction site. A variety of skilled tradespersons engaged on semirepetitive projects are less likely to be so easily supervised.

Hand tools account for a large percentage of the installation work. Pliers, screwdrivers, wrenches, and hammers are typical staples of the construction worker's tool pouch. An endless series of heterogeneous hand movements and individual decisions at the point of production are hallmarks of all levels of the building industry. While such unsu- pervised roles are common to skilled white-collar personnel in many industries, the typical world of blue-collar work operates with careful regulation and monitoring.

Technical and bureaucratic systems of job management and control typify the structure of American industrial relations. Similarly, the con- struction sector has adopted combinations of these methods, but still holds on to vestiges of its earlier relations. Clearly, the history of work practices must be considered in terms of workers' responses and unionization. Workers in the skilled building trades have been respon- sible for the formation of some of the strongest and most enduring trade unions in American history.

The unique experiences of tradespeople created workplace ties that brought about collective action. The wholesale movement of construc- tion from independent artisans and part-time tradespersons into a sys- tem of contract construction marked the rise of the modern building industry. As wage labor and competition emerged as central features of the late-nineteenth-century construction industry, workers increasingly sought protection from the uncertainties of free market construction. The Knights of Labor was the institution of choice early on, and that experience paved the way for the American Federation of Labor.

The rich economic history of the building industry is anchored to the people and technologies that have shaped it. While cutting-edge manufacturing plants operate with futuristically designed work spaces, construction still operates with remnants of a colorful and glorious past. The modern project continues to unfold with an appearance of chaos that eventually gives way to an orderly finished structure. Sidewalk superintendents remain perplexed by the juxtaposition of idle workers standing by a man-hoist and a crew high above them struggling to unload equipment from a crane's hook and arm. These are the same type of scenes that have been repeated across the vast time continuum of construction, save for the modern innovations of the foreman's time book and the worker's never-ending search for overtime.

CHAPTER 2

Economic Theory and the Construction Industry

Economic theory serves as a useful guideline for understanding the inner workings of a particular industry. In a study of construction operations, theory can be akin to a blueprint, providing direction and instruction on how diverse elements fit together. Similar to the blueprint that carries the engineer's initialed revisions, theory is capable of denoting changes and shifts in the economy. The following very generalized theoretical explanations will provide the reader with a choice of economic principles that may be applied to the modern construction industry. Following the format of Robert Heilbroner and Lester Thurow's classic introduction to economics in *Economics Explained,* this chapter will provide a progression of economic thought as it might apply to the building industry. Thus Adam Smith, Karl Marx, and John Maynard Keynes will all get their due over the next several pages.

As a champion of the free market, Smith discovered a system of emergent capitalism replete with small units of capital and nascent technological developments. His analysis drew heavily on assumptions about unfettered markets and the internal strength of a balanced system. Smithian principles can explain much about the workings of the modern construction market. Supply and demand equalities, the division of labor, and expectations of stable growth are all consistent with the economics of the construction industry. Equally important, the same analytical framework can be applied to the markets that interact with the construction industry. From this perspective, construction is viewed as part of a unified system of production, consumption, and distribution. The lingering theoretical question is this: Just how fully does Smith fully explain modern construction business cycles, with their rapid boom-and-bust movements?

Theoretically, Smithian construction firms produce in unrestricted markets in which the competition to become the low-cost producer serves as the great leveler. The known market price of a good is the target price at which all producers aim. Construction firms must endeavor to produce a finished installation at this going market rate.

Prices for Smith are regulated by "the proportion between the quantity which is actually brought to market and the demand of those who are willing to pay natural prices of the commodity" (Smith 1977 [1776], p. 151). Movements in supply and effective (money-backed) demand determine the price of an installation at a given moment. In the end, market participants reach mutually satisfactory prices that have the appearance of being naturally constrained (i.e., as if they were guided by an "invisible hand"). Too many contractors cause prices to fall perilously low, while too few contractors force prices to exorbitant heights. Built-in stability is the yield of a free market system, and the insurance for stability is competition.

In the early periods of capitalism, competition took on particular forms. Localized markets produced information on prices and production techniques that was available to all producers. Smith noted that while secrets in manufacture might be secure, it was hard to keep secrets in trade (1977, p. 163). Construction was typically carried out by a number of firms with enormous similarities.

Competition was focused on the productivity of individual producers. In the eighteenth century an individual's output was guided largely by knowledge, tools, and physical abilities. All firms were restricted by virtually the same physical limitations. With the absence of mechanization and the dependence on hand operations, masters were hard-pressed to apply additional units of labor to existing amounts of capital. The influence of diminishing returns was well under way.

Smith's realization that employers had adopted a novel technique to increase output is one of his significant contributions to economic history. What Smith described as the division of labor amounted to the rationalization of the eighteenth-century work force. For the construction industry, even today such a concept takes on an unusual significance.

The division of labor was essentially a description of the reorganization of the production process into a series of unique operations. Whereas goods were sometimes produced wholly by one draftsperson, the fragmentation of hand operations improved skill and dexterity. Repetition and familiarity were coupled with an increasing number of tasks in an attempt to raise productivity. The rising returns in the form of higher levels of output for the same amount of labor inputs simply reduced the unit costs of production.

The late-twentieth-century construction industry still has its roots in the job divisions of early capitalism. The general division of construction projects into building components (e.g., plumbing or carpentry) is a weak reference to the division of labor Smith was describing. The best examples are found within the trades themselves.

The work force on a large project is typically made up of gangs or crews. Deck gangs, riser gangs, and bull gangs are slang terms for particular aspects of any construction installation. The specific advantages of these divisions are most evident in the day-to-day operations of a deck gang.

The electrician's deck crew on a new high-rise housing development serves as an excellent example of the benefits derived from the division of labor. Electrical workers install conduit and boxes in the reinforcing rod and plywood forms prior to the pouring of the concrete deck. Speed and accuracy become crucial elements to the flow of the job. Deck work must be completed by the time concrete is delivered to the site, and errors in concrete work can become expensive change orders.

To ensure proper installation, foremen use repetitive job assignments. This has the twofold effect of increasing speed and reducing mistakes. Residential construction schedules are based on repetitive floor plans, and layouts are quickly mastered by skilled workers. The materials for the concrete phase of the project are spread out on the decking for the individual worker, thus eliminating the need to stop and replenish parts and fittings.

The resulting speed provides the electrical contractor with a series of choices. As completion time for a typical deck begins to decrease, workers are reassigned or terminated. The key factor here is that construction productivity can be enhanced by a 200-year-old technique that fits well with the hand-tool nonmechanized character of the industry. Unfortunately, as Smith was quick to point out, nonmechanized firms competing in this fashion would soon be pushing at the outer limits of their productivity frontiers.

The challenge for early capitalist producers was to surpass these limits. The natural course of development was in the sphere of technology. Skilled eighteenth-century hand labor, well managed and cleverly divided, was being augmented with machinery and labor-saving devices. The industrial revolution opened the flood gates of machine-assisted manufacturing, and industry would never be the same. Yet construction was not readily swept up with the torrent of innovation.

Heterogeneity, worker recalcitrance, and project size and duration all worked against mechanization. The engineering and logistical challenges of developing machinery to substitute for customized hand craftsmanship were, in the earliest stages of the industry's development, largely insurmountable. The modern era is not much different. Labor-saving devices such as robots or computers are used only minimally. Rather, it is the use of new materials, off-site fabrication, and improved training that help to extend the construction firm's productivity horizon.

Smith's vision of early capitalism is in many respects alive and well in the modern construction industry. The notion of growth through market stability is, of course, a popular modern economic theme. While construction employment, output, and productivity have long-run upward trends, construction as a sector of the economy is still battered by the boom–bust nature of cyclical investment. Does Smith's invisible hand really explain these inner workings? Does the division of labor provide economic efficiency, or is it primarily a management tool that leads to a deskilled and fragmented labor force?

To investigate these issues and to further join economic theory with modern construction reality, it is worthwhile to consider the theoretical perspective of Karl Marx. The appeal of Marx for a student of the construction industry is that Marx can provide a revealing alternative view of the dynamics at the point of production. If Smith's stability is not always apparent, then maybe Marx's world of struggle and crisis can lead to a more complete understanding of investment, employment, and productivity. In expounding on the "nature and causes of wealth," Smith found that self-interested parties (e.g., workers, contractors, and suppliers) are constrained by market competition. This has the effect of creating an orderly and stable industrial environment. On the contrary, Marx's investigation of wealth unfolds from a study of the focal point of the market system—the commodity. In a system of commodity exchange, all items natural and man-made become objects of desire not merely for their use value but for their exchange values as well.

On the construction site a multitude of commodities is produced during the building process. Embodied within these items are their exchange values, which have been created during the usual and customary time necessary for their construction. Thus the completed installation of a heating and ventilation system has exchange value that is of considerable interest to both the heating and ventilation contractor and the owner of the structure. The contractor sells the job to the owner, who in turn charges rents or sells parts of the structure. It is this exchange value that forms the basis for a final price.

Construction then serves as part of the free-market enterprise system in that it is the sector creating wealth in the form of finished construction products. Possession of these commodities themselves, or of their monetary equivalents, becomes the hallmark of wealth. It does not matter for the moment whether the value is embodied in the commodity form, or in its abstract representation—money. An individual's wealth would be considered the same regardless of whether he possessed a warehouse of plumbing supplies, an office tower, or money in the bank, providing these were of equivalent value.

Marx provides a single and unified schematic to demonstrate how this point of accumulation is reached. He defines a circuit of capital in which a sum of money (value) is exchanged for labor power and capital. The combining of the two indicates production, which results in commodities that are in turn sold in the market. For the process to be successful, these goods must be exchanged for a sum of value greater than the initial amount used for the purchase of capital and labor.

The circuit appears as this:

$$M < {}^{C}_{L} \ldots P \ldots C - M'$$

where M represents the contractor's original investment. A carpentry contractor would take her first sum of money and purchase the necessary capital (C) and labor (L) in order to erect walls, ceilings, and so forth. The contractor must then enter into an exchange of money for commodities and labor power. The costs associated with material become part of the cost of production while tools and machinery are accounted for to the extent of their usage.

The money exchange for the services of labor is of considerable importance from this perspective. The implication is that buyers and sellers of labor power meet freely in the market for those services and a wage bargain is struck. In the building trades there are a number of variations in the way labor power is bought and sold. Generally, hourly rates are agreed upon with stipulations about overtime or holidays. Union agreements establish collective rates for the remuneration of the covered workers. Regardless of the terms (with the exception of "lumping," where the worker shares in the final outcome of the job), labor power is bought and sold in a fashion similar to any other commodity. The hourly rates and conditions of employment have historically been affected by the level of unemployment, the demand for labor, and the productivity of individual workers. Thus, for Marx there is the historic "appearance" of a fair exchange underscoring such time-worn phrases as "a fair day's work for a fair day's pay."

Assuming that the contractor is a successful bidder and is able to purchase the requisite labor and materials, the next phase is production (P). Human labor then acts upon the building materials with workers pouring concrete, running pipe, and laying brick. Piles of sheetrock, skids of fixtures, and bundles of conduit are given a new usefulness by virtue of their installation. The items are cut, shaped, connected, and bent, growing in value as the workers' skills become embodied in the final product. In the modern sense, the employer's notion of value added comes to mind. In the Marxian system there is the added market constraint requiring that this work be completed in the agreed upon time frame, which is itself subject to competitive pressures.

The result of all of this effort—which includes the manager's planning, the foreman's direction, the mechanic's hand operations—is the commodity. It need not be recognizable as the sum total of individual units of labor and capital. The office tower is hardly reminiscent of the reams of material that lay outside the open hole prior to the foundation work. Nor does the building remind one of the human effort devoted to its construction, whether this skill be the entrepreneurial effort or the manual dexterity exerted on the site. What is of importance is that the final installation represent a consolidation of value into a marketable commodity.

The fact that so much construction takes place on a contractual basis does not alter the concept of value. What may become an issue is the price. Has the job been finished on time? What about additional labor time? Who will pay for the cost over-runs? This sets the stage for the final and in some respects most crucial segment of the circuit schematic, for at this point the entrepreneur attempts to sell the commodity. Ask contractors of any trade what the hardest part of their job is and they invariably answer "getting paid!"

In manufacturing, if all of these conditions are successfully met, then the owner of the final product must locate a buyer. In the building industry, custom work is done with the buyer already committed (important exceptions to this are home and speculative office construction). The issue at the end is likely to be agreement on the formal provisions of the contract. The quality of workmanship, timeliness, and warranty of the installation can all become boondoggles in closing out a job. Last but not least is M'. For the employer, the sale price must be one that exceeds the initial capital invested at the beginning of the circuit.*

For all of the novelty of Marx's exposition, there is at first glance the appearance that Smith's reliance on market mechanisms could easily be the cure for any problems in this circuit. However, there is not merely a question of the fragility of the circuit but of the tendency within that circuit toward breakdown. Two key aspects of the circuit move constantly toward destabilizing the flow of commodities.

The upshot of this schematic explanation is that the entire production of additional value is contingent on a most curious marketable commodity—labor power. Marx claims that the unique feature of labor power is that in a given day it can create more value than it consumes. One could argue, then, that the source of contractor profits is the ability of the tradespersons to create a finished product, the value of which exceeds the costs of replenishing those skills and abilities used up during production.

This built-in condition of the labor process allows the worker to lay claim to the surplus that has been produced, although ownership of the finished product (structure) is squarely in the hands of the owners of the means of production. In the construction industry, such a claim would lead to Marx's notion of class struggle in the form of refusing to sell one's labor power, organizing the unorganized, or shop-floor militancy in order to gain a greater share of the wealth.

Such scenarios were described by Marx in a period devoid of either labor mediation or a legal framework to establish workers' rights. The

*In value terms, $M' > M$, and $M' - M$ = surplus or, loosely, profit.

labor disputes of the late nineteenth century and early twentieth century often ended violently, with severe consequences for the workers and their families. From this perspective, the struggle over the length of the working day, the intensity of the labor effort, the conditions of employment, and, of course, the level of remuneration defined the separation between capital and labor.

The final comment on the Marxian paradigm focuses on the intended uses of M'. Let us agree, for example, that in round one all goes well and developers find suitable sites, contractors find qualified workers, and contented workers build a usable structure. Once the profit or surplus value is realized, a second round of production flows only from the entrepreneurial decision-making process. How much should be reinvested? Should there be an expansion of the firm's market share? What level of risk should the firm take in employing new personnel and garnering new business?

The building industry is subject to sharp fluctuations for a variety of reasons. The critical arguments developed by nontraditionalists apply a logic to the necessary conditions of production. If all these presuppositions for the building industry are realized, then growth is a possible outcome. If there is a breakdown at any of the points in the schematic, then growth is stymied. What is probably the most significant factor for the construction industry is the fact that the demand for its services is a derived demand. Markets such as housing, public works, and commercial construction need flows from other major economic sectors. Thus breakdowns and booms in related markets can produce major shifts in construction business patterns.

The ever-present concern for slowdown and recession in the overall economy gave rise to an entirely new strand of economic thought in the 1930s. Keynesian economic doctrine had a clear and profound effect on the building industry and offers a third view of the economics of this sector. A public policy reliance on the Keynesian perspective has led to the dramatic rise in government sector construction spending in the post–World War II era.

The historical focal point in this case is the Great Depression of the 1930s. The economic vibrancy of the 1920s quickly collapsed, shattering the expectations of a generation and reshaping political and economic attitudes across the Western world. As could be expected, the construction industry followed suit. Construction employment had tumbled nationwide. Building tradesmen migrated across the states in search of employment. Union membership roles were shaken and the limited legal status of organizing left the worker at a decided disadvantage. Recessions and depressions were not unfamiliar occurrences. The business cycle had produced severe downturns in 1908, 1912, and 1914. Conversely, the booms of 1918 and the more recent expansion of the 1920s had led to a fair degree of economic euphoria. Such economic giddiness as was found in the Roaring Twenties was not wholly supported by the historical events of the time.

Theories on the causes of the Great Depression have often pointed to a long list of culprits. Credit purchases, margin stock buying, and political ineptitude are a few that come readily to mind. Yet a plausible economic explanation can help to demonstrate how the construction industry is buffeted by exogenous economic activity.

As general investment levels collapsed during the 1930s, an already sluggish national construction industry slipped further into a disastrous slump. Construction output had fallen by 26 percent in 1930, 29 percent in 1931, and 47 percent in 1932 (McElvaine 1984, p. 74). The gloomy statistical reports included a drop in construction output of 78 percent from 1929 to the economic trough of 1933.

Where was the invisible hand when the world so desperately needed it? Had the circuit of capital finally snapped, irreparably damaged by reluctant possessors of surplus value and the inability to drive wages of all types below their subsistence levels? Classical economics and the all-encompassing corollary known as Say's Law (supply creates its own demand) fell short in accounting for the weakness in demand for what little supply was being produced.

One plausible explanation of the Great Depression is worth noting. The underlying cause can be attributed to the concept of underconsumption, where output far outpaces effective demand. In such a situation inventories rise, wages are flat, and overproduction causes shutdowns in the production process itself.

The historical prelude reverts to the end of World War I and the breaking of militant trade unions. Following the Palmer raids of the post–World War I era and the rise of company unionism, "millions of American workers had to suffer the low pay and long hours of the open shop for eighteen more years" (Boyer and Morais 1982, p. 209).

The low wages were matched by an incredible 52.5 percent rise in productivity from 1917 to 1927 (Boyer and Morais 1982, p. 237). Mass production of the automobile and household appliances had led to an extensive array of consumer products (Palmer and Colton 1965, p. 778). Yet working-class household incomes could not keep pace with output, leaving Keynes to suggest that neither Smith nor Say could account for the magnitude of the market failure.

Contract construction employment had begun to decline steadily beginning in 1928 and did not return to the earlier levels for another thirteen years (U.S. Department of Commerce 1978, Table G1-H, p. 24). The inability of producers to reduce inventories provided little incentive to commit additional funding toward capital investments. Without economic growth there would be a steady downward trend in the demand for construction worker skills.

Keynes's salvation of free enterprise hinged on the adjustment process among demand, employment, and investment. His critique zeroed in on the concept of the real wage bargain, arguing that the workers reacted based on assumptions about money wages. Profit-squeezed employers would begin a process of driving money wages downward in order to reduce production costs. Unfortunately, the successful lowering of workers' wages also drove down consumption demand and built up resistance from employees toward any further reduction in the level of money wages.

Keynes essentially argued that a shortfall in the demand in the form of savings could create full employment, but that this is not an automatic adjustment caused by a flexible money wage. Employment is determined by the propensity to consume and the rate of new investment (Keynes 1964 [1937], p. 38). Without further employment, there is no increase in consumption and thus no basis for economic expansion. Hence, without the potential for future profits, there is no investment. In such a situation the system runs the risk of permanent stagnation at best.

How, then, does Keynes find a willing investor without upsetting the rules of market economics? He turns to an exogenous influence, namely the public sector. It is left to the government to stimulate the economy through public expenditures. As money is pumped into the system through construction projects, roadwork, or agricultural programs, consumption will rise. The twofold effect is to raise business expectation about future profits and, more importantly, to begin a demand-induced rise in prices. If money wages remain at rock-bottom levels and prices move upward, then real wages decline. This makes workers a relatively cheap and attractive factor of production. Once stimulated by the potential for low wages and higher prices, the business sector is then capable of generating further investment, which will fuel a recovery.

The legacy of Keynes for the construction industry is the massive influx of public sector capital investments and the increasing state role in monitoring the industry. The Keynesian influence is found in projects as diverse as the Tennessee Valley Power Authority and the World Trade Center in New York. Government financing became an integral part of contractors' and developers' rational business expectations by developing a significant source of construction demand. At the same time, legislative issues and administrative bodies parallel the growth of governmental construction outputs.

It is not immediately clear whether one of these theoretical positions champions over the other two. Rather, it is more useful to note that all three positions possess a powerful internal logic that provides keen insights into market operations years after the authors have passed on. As this text moves through more general descriptions of the multibillion-dollar construction industry, each of these perspectives will provide a solid foundation for analysis.

CHAPTER 3

An Industry Overview

It is not difficult to get a sense of the fragmentation of the construction industry. A walk down a busy big-city block where buildings are under construction is usually very revealing. Multimillion-dollar structures are erected by large-volume contractors only a few yards from small-scale projects that are handled by one- or two-person shops. This dual economic structure is by no means foreign to the American economy as a whole. What is unique is that the two are participants within the same industry. How they coexist and compete is to a large extent shaped by the structure of the construction industry.

In 1992, the Census of Construction Industries reported that there were nearly 2 million businesses operating in the construction industry. The fact that 1.3 million of these firms, proprietorships, and partnerships were without payrolls reflects the tremendous diversity in markets and organization. Of firms with payrolls, 50 percent had fewer than five employees, and the 214,000 firms with more than five employees accounted for approximately 80 percent of the value of construction activity.

In 1993 there were 598,255 construction shops employing a total of over 4 million people. Of these, nearly 83 percent had fewer than ten employees (U.S. Department of Commerce, *County Business Patterns,* 1993). The breakdown of companies by numbers of employees as shown in Table 3.1 reflects not only the stable structure of the industry but the types of markets for construction services.

To emphasize the slowness of change in the structure of firm organization, it is worth noting figures from prior census reports. The 1967 census reported 795,000 construction establishments, 426,000 of these without payrolls. Five years later, in 1972, the Bureau of the Census

Table 3.1

Establishment Size in the Construction Industry, 1993

Employees Per Firm	Number of Firms	Total Employees
1–4	388,034	610,284
5–9	106,284	696,031
10–19	59,439	792,488
20–49	32,356	955,048
50–99	8,152	551,002
100–249	3,157	459,062
250–499	615	207,210
500–999	159	104,863
1,000 or more	59	148,122

Source: U.S. Department of Commerce, Bureau of the Census, *County Business Patterns,* United States Summary (Washington, D.C.: Government Printing Office, 1993).

reported growth to 921,000 firms—again with more than 50 percent without paid employees. In 1972, 80 percent of the firms had less than 10 employees.

Construction firms appear as a mind-boggling array of different-sized units of capital. Proverbial Mom-and-Pop shops are typical participants in alteration and small-scale building projects. In these situations the employer is often estimator, expediter, and installer while family members work as bookkeepers and occasional helpers.

Often these shops are not unionized and are subject to intense price competition while operating with thin profit margins. Market entry for such firms involves relatively low capital investments. Licensing provides a minor hurdle, as do insurance and bonding to guarantee fiscal responsibility. For many employers, the relatively low start-up costs are strong inducements for going out on one's own. Of course, productivity in construction can be largely related to individual hourly outputs; therefore, numbers of employees coupled with hours of employment provide a clue to the thinness of the profit margin. Self-employed proprietors or partners are limited by physical hourly limits and the industry-average levels of outputs.

Small companies are readily contrasted with contractors employing upward of several hundred employees. Such firms may be privately or publicly owned, and may operate within several states or on an international scale. The markets that they enter can easily cross between public and private, and often represent mixes between residential and commercial properties.

Internally, these firms are departmentalized. Estimation, engineering, drafting, and installation are specific areas of responsibility within the firm. Some of the larger or more ambitious specialty companies will undertake the role of prime contractor, thereby serving as the project manager in one instance while operating as a contractor in another.

Profitability could be a closely held secret among firms and partners, or could be a matter of record in a publicly traded corporation. The bottom lines of Fluor-Daniel, for example, are found in its annual reports, while the Tishman Construction Company remains a large but privately held corporation. The available information indicates that the returns are substantially greater to firms over a certain threshold size (see Cassimatis 1969). For example, in 1964, only 0.0005 percent of all construction firms were responsible for 19.2 percent of the sector's output (Cassimatis 1969, p. 35, Table 2.20). Similarly, in 1992 shops employing five or more employees were only 11 percent of all construction establishments but "accounted for more than 80 percent of the total value of business done" (U.S. Department of Commerce, *Census of Construction Industries*, U.S. Summary 1992).

While many large and small firms are involved with a variety of jobs, there are also specialty shops that have secured a niche in the market. One concrete firm may focus almost exclusively on sidewalk installations while others will become associated with block work or foundations. A particular plumbing contractor will consistently be a subcontractor to a particular architect/interior designer while another may only install and maintain hospital plumbing systems. Repetition, personal relationships, and quality control are important features of successful competitors. By carving out a defined piece of the marketplace, smaller firms can withstand the intense competitive pressures associated with small-scale construction projects.

Despite size differentials, many firms compete in several construction markets. The markets can be roughly divided into private residential, private commercial (nonresidential), and public construction. The kind of work these categories include ranges from alterations to existing structures to new construction work. These divisions are adequate for instructional purposes, but there are in practice a variety of cases in which these distinctions have been blurred (e.g., the World Trade Center was built with Port Authority money but considerable portions of the space are leased to private enterprises).

Residential construction has always been one of the mainstays of the construction industry. Housing starts are typically cited as an indicator of the vibrancy of the overall economy. In 1992 single-family home building and apartment construction comprised a 60-billion-dollar industry. In 1994 alone it is estimated to that nearly one-half of the general contracting labor force was employed on residential projects (U.S. Department of Commerce, *Construction Review,* Winter 1995–1996). Private residential housing includes one-family units, attached dwellings, and multi-apartment structures.

In general, housing falls into the durable goods category. The endurance of residential dwellings depends on a large number of variables. Weather, materials, and location are historically key determinants of housing longevity. Hundred-year-old tenements survive on the Lower East Side of New York City while numerous colonial dwellings still stand intact along the eastern seaboard. Modern collateralized home mortgages are standard financial instruments running in lengths of fifteen to thirty years. All of these factors point toward a market that is clearly not concerned with planned obsolescence.

It is this durability that causes investment in the housing industry to be strongly linked with expansion rather than replacement. Homebuilding cycles have been related to demographic shifts and movements in the general economic cycle. Waves of immigration have successively pushed for urban housing while industrialization produces domestic migration to suburban and rural areas. The entire notion of the bedroom community is a phenomenon of modern industrialized life.

The demand for housing and the pricing structure of the market require certain efficiencies in the construction phase. Generally, homes can be built rapidly, even in the case of the custom-built dwelling. The economies necessary to maintain profitability are found in the construction industry's answer to the garment center's off-the-rack suit.

The single-family housing development, the condominium-townhouse community, and the high-rise apartment building have certain things in common. Repetition in design and installation produces the speed and productivity necessary to satisfy the effective demand for housing. Variation takes place in the apartment house line (e.g., the "a" line or "b" line), individual structures have repetitive styles (Cape Cod, etc.), while attached housing varies by using the mirror image or unique angles.

Workers become adept at fulfilling the requirements for each specific task, and general skills are utilized from project to project. Framing, roughing, and concrete are basic building procedures that change only relative to the materials at hand. Techniques for concrete high-risers are standardized, while wood-frame homes are the exclusive domain of certain firms and their employees.

The need for efficiency is imposed by the nature of the housing cycle. Its boom–bust style dictates the presence of an almost unpredictable economic clock whose time can readily run out on the builder halfway through construction. Interest rate sensitivity and cash flow from sales are significant factors in pushing a project to completion. Interest rates can stymie sales or squeeze the builder on a construction loan. Indeed, rapid rate rises on loans after construction has started can bring work on a building or a development to a grinding halt. As well, a downturn in the market can crimp sales, effectively cutting off funding for the next segment of construction. The *Wall Street Journal* noted that the credit crunch of 1993 exerted a veritable "choke hold" on home builders, with only the top quality and the most secure builders able to qualify for funding (Carlton 1993). Small and mid-sized builders are vulnerable to such mundane factors as bank-lending attitudes (Carlton and Pacelle 1992).

Thus while the housing market is historically a key influence on the level of new construction, it is relatively unstable and speculative. It is instructive to contrast the residential segment of the industry with its somewhat more glamorous counterparts in the nonresidential sectors. Private, nonresidential construction encompasses commercial projects of every size and use imaginable. From "taxpayers" (one-story rows of commercial space) to sleek, gleaming office towers, private investment provides the stimulus to huge portions of the construction market.

Historically, the bulk of commercial projects has been carried out by employers engaged in contract construction. The term *contract* implies that the firm will agree to provide the specific labor requirements necessary to perform the installation. The alternative method, which seems to remain fairly stable at about 10 percent of the entire construction work force, is known as force account work (Cassimatis 1969). In such cases, larger employers such as a utility or a major corporation will direct their own employees in the construction of internal projects.

Annually, nonmanufacturing commercial structures comprise up to

40 percent of the nonresidential building in the United States (*Engineering News-Record* [hereafter *ENR*], January 25, 1993, p. 36). Within this category, office structures and retail space explain nearly 35 percent of construction projects in current dollars. The high-rise innovations of the nineteenth century have continued to play an important role in twentieth-century building patterns. The preference for the high-rise is a reflection of the overall business climate for developers and corporations, who often vie for locations, labor, and materials.

Manufacturing construction expenditures are functions of investment for particular industries. Plant modernization and inventory-based investment are as capable as a general economic expansion of fueling a construction boom. Yet the direction of real manufacturing expenditure has been decidedly negative in the late twentieth century as American manufacturing industries continue to decline.

Commercial construction can be differentiated by the sources of funding. Speculative projects such as unrented office towers or empty storefronts are generally financed through the establishment of lines of credit or direct construction loans. As such, the builders and therefore the subcontractors and their workers are vulnerable to fluctuations in interest rates and government fiscal policies.

Corporate building, whether intended for mixed use or as a company headquarters, will often use allocations of internal funding to ensure completion of the project. This helps to minimize the effects of interest rates and public policies. Of course, disastrous conditions such as the stock market crash of 1987 can lead to the instantaneous halting of a construction program, as was the case for the L.F. Rothschild brokerage firm office project in downtown Manhattan. The scale of major construction projects often presents itself as a barrier to small and mid-sized firms. High-rise office towers may require bonded bidders, access to a large work force, and a proven track record in a particular aspect of the industry. Capital requirements in terms of tools and material further reduce the number of firms capable of entering the high-rise new construction and renovation markets.

Commercial projects can also be differentiated from residential projects by the complexity of the installations. Time and money are saved in residential construction through repetition in design and application. Workers improve their skills and speed through repetitive operations. Speculative commercial spaces are often constructed for the general market without a specific tenant. Once the core is completed, the offices may be custom designed and erected by the on-site contractor or an alternative firm, thereby reducing the efficiencies created by using the same firm throughout the project.

Custom work, control systems, or new technologies (e.g., data communications) can provide a competitive advantage for an entire set of specialized firms. However, the intricacies of this type of work can lead to longer installation times. This raises serious issues about construction productivity since the advantages of repetition are lost for unique projects.

Commercial construction is not limited to new installations, but extends to a vast spectrum of alteration work. Specialty contractors and subcontractors enter markets as competitive as those in the one- and two-family housing industry. This segment of the construction industry, while often mistakenly associated with only large-scale projects, is actually composed of two distinct segments. One revolves around new construction jobs; the other focuses on renovation and alteration. In part, this explains how large, heavily capitalized firms can come to compete with small Mom-and-Pop type operations despite being based in two distinct markets.

The final area of the industry that needs to be reviewed is the public sector. The historic functions of government and the Keynesian legacy of governmental expenditure have fueled an extensive array of public projects. While the scale and type of construction in the public sector are similar to that found in residential and commercial projects, pay rates, bidding procedures, and contract awards are subject to a much more complex network of laws and regulations. Public works projects can range from sewage treatment plants to the renovation of patient rooms in a public hospital. Such undertakings are often responsible for improving and maintaining the infrastructure of the nation. Road work, bridge and tunnel construction, and transit systems consume large portions of public capital budgets.

Public contract construction can be found at the traditional three levels of the public sector. Federal, state, and local authorities have bidding requirements mandating construction work to be conducted under legislated guidelines. Regardless of the source of the expenditure, there is an economic impact for each specific locale. Clearly, public works provide employment for workers and revenues for employers in the same fashion as private investment. What most clearly distinguishes public from private investment is the decision-making process behind the respective outlays.

Capital expenditures by public authorities may be appropriated by legislative bodies or may be authorized by voter initiatives such as bond issues. A network of grant-in-aid and regulatory commissions is often charged with the management of particular projects. For example, the physical plant of the New York City public school system had decayed to the point where public debate resulted in the creation of a School Construction Authority. Legislative discussions on the same issue led to a revamping of the way in which school projects were to be awarded and managed.

Public construction programs are also subject to wage regulation, which establishes prevailing labor rates for certain trades. The awarding authority is required to solicit contract bids based on these wage rates. The particular rates are established by a legislated formula that is generally based on average and historical area rates.

The federal prevailing rates are established under the Davis–Bacon Act, which was enacted in 1931 in order to limit the incursion of itinerant contractors into depressed local markets. By standardizing wage rates based on the prevailing area pay scales, local contractors could not be undercut by employers from other low-waged localities. At the same, the federal government was attempting to extract an area level of quality that could not be reduced by the payment of substandard wages. Numerous states have adopted similar measures since the passage of Davis–Bacon.

Construction at all levels of the public sector remains a critical component of the industry's local outputs. In 1995, new public sector construction put in place was measured to be worth 142.8 billion dollars, or a little more than one-quarter of all new construction activity (U.S. Department of Commerce, *Construction Review,* Fall–Winter 1995–96, p. 1, Table 1). Federal construction expenditures totaled 15.5 billion dollars while state and local construction totaled 127 billion dollars.

When the public sector is combined with the private sector, the entire domestic building industry is capable of creating millions of job opportunities in a given year. According to the Bureau of Labor Statistics, there were 5.1 million people employed in contract construction of which 4 million were actual construction employees (U.S. Department of Commerce, *Construction Review,* Summer 1995). The building trades are unionized by individual crafts and the unionized markets have distinguishable characteristics from the nonunion markets.

Legally, there are no special restrictions that prohibit union organizing in particular construction markets. Organizing must be conducted within the framework of the National Labor Relations Act. What adds considerably to the complexity of the union issue are factors such as market structure and institutional influences.

The housing market and the levels of union strength in a particular geographic area can help to determine the nature of market labor relations. Profit margins for single-family dwellings may make union organization efforts fruitless, while the possibility of securing economic wage rents in the high-rise luxury housing market can lead to strong union commitments and project agreements to hire union building specialty workers.

Commercial construction markets are influenced by institutional as well as market forces. The success of union workers in securing employment on certain projects can be related to the unified strength of all the trades as well as the additional consideration of whether the project owner is a unionized shop itself. While Coors was a nonunion beer producer, it often would use union labor on construction projects in deference to the union strength among the skilled trades in the area. There are also many large unionized corporations and manufacturers that routinely accept union construction labor as a condition of having a unionized industrial work force (e.g., General Motors).

While labor forces in industrial union markets can fit general job descriptions, union construction labor strictly mirrors the special skills required by the contractors. Union jurisdictional agreements, clearly defined work rules, and job conditions spell out the description of employees' responsibilities. Where disputes take place, mechanisms such as labor councils are generally in place, while the rule of historic precedent usually supports the trade that has traditionally performed the work. As Daniel Mills (1972b) has noted, flexibility is the key to resolving any disagreement since projects are of a short duration.

Skilled trades offer apprenticeship opportunities as market-entry positions, and these programs are formalized through state-run boards. Union market labor is also expanded through the efforts of union organizing drives; the peaks and troughs of membership numbers are subject to the ups and downs of the work picture. Union membership is associated with strong labor attachment and a wide range of benefits, annuities, pensions, and significant wage premiums, all of which are lacking in the nonunion market.

Nonunion labor markets are subject to wide variations in pay rates and skills (Bourdon and Levitt 1980, chap. 3). Since there is little formal training, employers must invest in search techniques that can overcome an inefficient signaling process. While union markets have access to hiring and referral halls, nonunion contractors must individually identify attributes that are important to their job-site needs. This creates a trial-and-error basis for employment, underscored by a new-hire probationary period. Wages are subject to the going rate and are negotiable at every hire. Larger nonunion employers tend to offer a wide range of health and welfare benefits, although these are seldom transportable, as they are in the union market.

A final note in the overview of construction markets should mention the existence of a large number of contractor associations. By size, these employer groups range from associations between the nation's largest general contractors to a loosely connected cohort of nonunion special trades employers. These organizations are active in political· campaigns, labor negotiations, and the dissemination of trade information. They are also important because they act as a response to the organizations in the labor market. However, these trade groups have a variety of rules and membership plans and often produce nonbinding resolutions for member firms. Associations comprised of unionized building trades contractors are more formally structured since they are often integrally involved in the collective bargaining process.

Despite the patterns of employment and business opportunity, the construction industry is subject to a variety of forces that have been reshaping the appearance of the building sector. While traditional stereotypes abound, it is worth considering the overview presented in this chapter along with many of the emerging trends in construction employment, business practice, and technology.

CHAPTER 4

Trends and Directions in
the Construction Industry

Fundamental change in the construction industry is seldom sweeping. It is often slow-paced and years can pass before practices become standardized across the national market. In part, the plethora of localized markets with their own traditions, codes, and special requirements have served to create a conservatism in construction methods.

There are, however, a number of new directions within the industry that represent deviations from this traditional history. Technological advances, shifts in firm structure, and a changing work force composition are elements that may alter the face (if not the entire corpus) of the industry. It is worth examining each of these facets with respect to the industry's needs and the dynamics of the wider macroeconomic system.

One of the few long-term measurements of construction output is the contribution of the construction industry to the Gross Domestic Product (GDP). Published by the U.S. Department of Commerce in the *Survey of Current Business,* the long-run trend in construction output is similar to the overall performance of the economy. Graphically, its historic direction has been upward and outward. The same is true regardless of whether nominal or real data are observed (see Figures 4.1 and 4.2). This is defined by the Department of Commerce as the gross product originating (GPO), value added, or simply an industry's gross output minus its intermediate inputs.

This is not to be confused with the arguments that extend to the issue of construction productivity. The productivity debate with respect to output per man-hour and the union/nonunion question will be addressed in chapters 8 and 9. While the trends in total output move

Figure 4.1. **Declining Portion of Real Construction GDP as Part of Total Real U.S. GDP, 1977–1993**

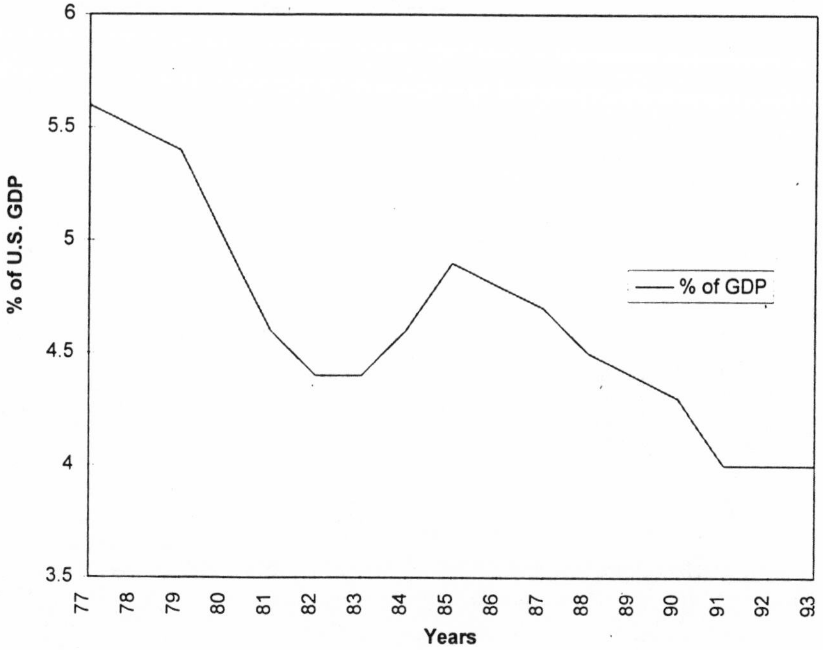

Source: Data from U.S. Department of Commerce, *Survey of Current Business,* November 1993.

steadily outward, it would suffice to say at this point that productivity measures are often ambiguous.

It is necessary to understand the traditional interdependence of the various trades and the cooperative nature of construction. The overall exigencies of a construction project require a smooth flow from phase to phase. Therefore, productivity enhancements in one sphere or trade can have spillover effects on a related one. Efficiencies in falsework construction can reduce labor hours for a host of trades, while advancements in concrete mixing or pouring can induce speed in the deck trades.

Much of the focus for raising productivity has centered on the heavy-construction segment of the industry. This primarily involves excavation and structural work. Improvements in machines or materials are seen as having a ripple effect throughout the remainder of the project. For example, increased speed in excavating a site allows erection to

Figure 4.2. **Comparison of Construction GDP and Total U.S. GDP, 1949–1993**

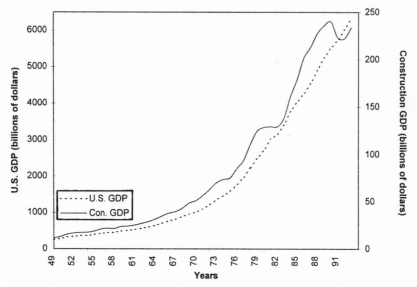

Source: Data from U.S. Department of Commerce, *Survey of Current Business,* November 1993, May 1993, April 1995.

proceed before the onset of adverse weather conditions. Thus, hoisting or earth-moving equipment manufacturers are locked into competitive research to develop greater load-bearing and more powerful dozing machines.

Improvements in pumping technology have allowed contractors to pump concrete to incredible heights. The Texas Commerce Tower in Houston was built with concrete pumped to just over 1,000 feet while the ninety-five-story Petronas Twin Tower in Malaysia had concrete pumped to over 1,400 feet at a rate of over 16 cubic yards per hour (*ENR*, January 20, 1995). The 1992 construction of the NCNB Bank Tower in Charlotte, North Carolina, created an 870-foot-high poured-in-place office structure featuring "48 foot column free spans from perimeter to core" (*ENR*, January 20, 1992, p. 46).

In the skilled mechanical trades, the movement has been toward increasingly sophisticated types of installations. The development of electronic controls that regulate and integrate a variety of home services (e.g., air-conditioning, security, and lighting) is indicative of innovations in building and home design. Theoretically, integrated systems of all types (electrical, communications, and heating ventilation) provide cost-efficient usage for the homeowner. In fact, the revolution in electronics has made it practical to center the control of a variety of appliances in one computerized base.

The development of fiber-optic cable has opened up the real possibility of mixed-voltage outlets for voice communication (telephony), data delivery (E-mail), and standard electric power. At the same time, more far-reaching concepts such as interactive communications have re-created the living room as an interactive retail outlet where television viewers will be able to see and virtually feel a product before making an on-line purchase.

The upshot of these innovations is that the mechanical building trades need to have the skills to install these types of features. New construction alteration and traditional trouble shooting must conform to the needs of future technologies. While the spheres of work have historically been separated by the customary division of labor by trade, employers and their employees find their work assignments more and more to be crossing the usual lines of demarcation.

Consistent with the issues of changing technologies and skills are noticeable shifts in the labor market. These are occurring in the structure and composition of the construction labor force, and can hardly be viewed as independent of social and market forces outside the construction industry. Competition among firms, the mix of construction output, the rise in double-income families, and the demands of minority workers have served to reconstitute a once traditional image of the building industry.

In 1972, Daniel Mills cited statistics indicating that the building trades were more than 40 percent unionized across the nation (Mills 1972b, pp. 16–17). Hard union data on the percentage of construction workers who are organized can be difficult to obtain due to the wide range of employers and the short duration of jobs. Yet by all accounts there has been a significant decrease in the union segment of the construction industry. Rather than the stalwart 40 percent, many union officials themselves have claimed to represent only 16 percent of the national construction labor market, while the 1995 Bureau of Labor Statistics (BLS) Household Data Survey estimated representation at 18.8 percent.

It is not immediately clear whether this is part of a cyclical pattern or a long-run trend. What is clear is that there has been a general decline in the proportion of private industry that is unionized, as well as an increase in building projects.

In his arguments on the productivity issue, Steven Allen (1985) noted the rising volume of single-family home construction and the geographic shift in demand. The one-family housing industry has historically been dominated by nonunion shops, while regional pockets of economic growth such as the Southwest are often underorganized relative to the large metro centers. Such swings in unionization may prove over time to be spikes or dips away from the actual long-run trend.

A more discernible direction is the rise in nonunion or open-shop construction. In open-shop firms, trade assignments are mixed with skills and responsibilities that are created as the need occurs. The lack of formal training and the establishment of general helper categories offer a flexibility in tasks that is absent in the narrowly defined job descriptions of the union shops.

Open shops have expanded their market share of construction on both large-scale commercial and residential projects. With pay scales that are significantly lower than union hourly rates, open shops have been a primary factor in the falling numbers of the unionized construction work force.

Along these lines has been a series of efforts to reshape or recall the federal prevailing wage legislation of the Davis–Bacon Act. Union labor has depended on the quality arguments surrounding this legislation while open shops have called it an impediment to competition. In the 1980s and 1990s there has been a general weakening of the legislation through amendments to the methods of calculation of the prevailing wage and the types of work covered under the law. The result is that this has added to the long-run decline in the union segment of the building market.

A more identifiable long-run movement is found in the changing composition of the work force. The particular focus in this case is on minority and female entrants into the labor market. Employment gains by nonwhite males have been strong for nearly thirty years, although not without difficulty and confrontation. In part, the rapid swings in the economy have served to intensify the competition for relatively well-paid construction jobs. The changing social climate of the 1960s and 1970s helped provide the impetus to legal and moral challenges to hiring barriers. Title VII of the 1964 Civil Rights Act is credited with providing the grounds for legal challenges to discrimination in the workplace while the Equal Opportunity Employment Commission is the agency of enforcement. Thus, boom periods have had to sustain expanding work opportunities or face increasing friction from within the labor market for a finite number of employment positions as well as a rising demand for market entrance.

The entry of nontraditional groups has been spurred by several factors. Simple market economics has made racial and sexual discrimination an inefficient means of searching for workers. The loss of output caused by failing to hire a capable worker cannot be rationally justified since it results in an income loss to the firm. While discriminatory hiring barriers may still confront the average worker, theoretically such barriers retard output, revenue, and profit by arbitrarily excluding potentially productive workers from the workplace.

In the case where unique skills must be acquired through a training or apprentice program, the state has stepped in on a number of levels. Antidiscrimination hiring plans such as the Philadelphia Plan of 1970 were initiated by the courts to ensure that training programs were not used as barriers to construction labor-market entry. A series of executive orders and state review of apprentice programs have been responsible for increasing minority participation in the industry. More recently, state executive orders have been directed at minority involvement on the employers' side. Thus, in addition to the states' efforts to seek minority employment, states have also developed a means to increase the work awarded to minority- and female-run businesses.

Finally, there has been a voluntary lowering or removal of the barriers to hiring and entrance into training programs. Without formally acknowledging past practices, unions and employers have sought to comply with representative percentages of minorities and women within their ranks.

The question of minority and female employment has a number of dimensions. Given the historical barriers to industry entry, there are two immediate questions that arise. The first is whether or not the industry has made measurable progress in opening beginning-level positions to the overall population. The second concerns the specific issues of gender. Has the trend for advancement of women of all races into the building trades been the same as that for minority men? What steps have contractors (union and nonunion) taken to create job-site atmospheres that remove discrimination or harassment? None of these questions has a definitive answer, but there are sufficient data to get a sense of the directions of career opportunities in the construction sector.

Several sources offer statistical data that can shed light on this topic. BLS employment reports from construction firms can include all employees or specify construction workers only. The BLS reported construction trade employment of 108,000 women in 1982 and 120,000 in 1995, an increase of 11 percent. Yet the real issue is not total construction employment but the number of tradespersons. A rise of 12,000 employees could be measuring office, engineering, or some other aspect of the firm's operations. The same BLS reports also showed a 29 percent increase in male employment during the same period, an 18 percent increase in black male employment, and a 14 percent decline in employment for white females. The apparent contradiction in statistics for women stems from the fact that the total employment category includes all employees—bookkeepers, secretaries, estimators, and engineers. A rise in office personnel could show an increase in female employment in spite of a declining white female field worker population.

One of the more telling signs of progress in the industry can be observed in union apprentice statistics. A common view about discrimination is that it occurs primarily in the union sector. Both Allen (1994) and Clinton Bourdon and Raymond Levitt (1980, chapter 4) have cited statistics to the contrary. Although there is a dismal hiring record in terms of inclusion, there has been significant progress in the union sector over the last several years.

A 1990 General Accounting Office survey of apprenticeship programs indicated that minority placement had risen by 50 percent since 1973. For the same period, the survey found that female participation rates of 7 percent did not reflect the nearly 50 percent labor-market rate of women across the nation (*ENR,* September 21, 1992, p. 13).

Apprentice programs are barred by law from discrimination based on race or gender. All programs must be part of an affirmative action plan, although variations exist in the scope and magnitude of the efforts. Despite these plans, a number of factors can come together to slow down minority and female participation rates.

To what might be considered its social or economic effects can be added the political dimension of affirmative action. A rising social consciousness beginning in the 1960s could agitate for greater employment opportunities, and a declining real-income effect for workers in the 1980s could increase the competition for decent-paying construction jobs. Yet the resolution of the needs of minority and female workers has become a significant political issue. This can revolve around pending legislation, lobbying, and public campaigning. It can also be demonstrated through the level of commitment to enforcement. In 1984, a review of minority and female advancement by McGraw-Hill's *Engineering News-Record* listed slow progress due to the "three Rs: recession, Reagan and reluctance" (*ENR*, September 20, 1984).

A crucial element in hiring practices is the demand for construction workers. In slack periods or recessions, the lower demand sharply reduces the number of openings in entry-level programs. Downturns in the economy have the twofold effect of constricting hiring in formal apprentice programs while lengthening the wait time on the supply queue for openings. This market mechanism reduces the potential number of applicants while lowering the overall demand for vocational training. Since downturns not only limit job opportunities but also dampen wage growth, careers in the affected trades become relatively less attractive.

The "Reagan factor," as it is termed, is not an indictment of the former president per se but rather refers to the influence of the executive office in enforcing the law. The claim is that the Equal Employment Opportunity Commission did not use its full offices to insist on affirmative action in the building industry as a priority. This inaction was then compounded by a curtailing of national progress reports on apprentice program composition. The net result was to weaken affirmative action administratively and then to inhibit the data collection that allowed an evaluation.

Nonenforcement is a political tool that has been used in a number of circumstances. In 1996 the Associated Builders and Contractors filed suit against Secretary of Labor Robert Reich for failure to implement data collection as it pertains to Davis–Bacon helper employment. The change in the use of helpers was developed in 1982 but was not initiated due to a pending judicial review and a lack of program funding. Helpers, as distinguished from apprentices, need not be trade specific and would establish a pay category distinct from both journeypersons and apprentices. The new rules call for a determination by the Department of Labor as to the prevalence of helper employment in a particular geographic area. Where the use of helpers was found to be prevailing, federal construction projects would be required to allow this new category of workers. Even after the restoration of funding, the actual surveys were not being conducted. This prompted open-shop employers to file suit to challenge the extent of discretionary administrative action by the Department of Labor.

This leaves the third "R" for reluctance. How well do unions, employers, builders, and other industry participants handle the problem of sexual and racial discrimination? Is there a process in place to deal with such issues, or is resolution left to the judgment of the site supervisors? Have the trades responded more favorably toward minority males than toward females as a group? There are also legal issues surrounding harassment and the growing reliance on judicial review for determinations and possible monetary awards.

Sketchy statistical results leave room for speculation as to differing trends in female and minority group employment. The statistics on female field employment are ambiguous. Channels of information about job openings for minority workers, pay, and employment conditions provide a relatively accurate depiction of what a new employee can expect (David M. Gordon 1974). If the economic and political influences work against recruitment, then there is little reason to think that job-site prejudices will dissipate. Thus, if both white and nonwhite women perceive the construction industry as being hostile to their employment, there will be a commensurate decline in female job applicants. In sum, we can tentatively conclude from data that minority males are being more readily absorbed into the culture of the construction industry than are females.

Female employment trends are paralleled by the sexual harassment issue. This is clearly not a construction-specific problem, but grows out of the competition for jobs and the ways that females and males relate to each other in the workplace. The commitment to ensuring a gender- or racially neutral work site is closely connected to supervisory sensitivity and training in the overall work force.

Companies may make every effort to comply with standards of workplace fairness. Policy statements, on-site meetings, and grievance procedures are important steps in diffusing potentially disruptive or litigious situations. To some extent, the unionized sector has an institutionalized framework in place for preventing frictional situations. The growing use of union-sponsored seminars and training classes provides a basis for creating job-site harmony. Since apprentice programs must set aside openings for female and minority applicants, the logic and cost incentives exist for developing a smooth training process. Non-union and open-market shops are certainly capable of establishing their own mechanisms for dealing with these issues. While meeting statutory hiring requirements for female and minority workers, an individual company could simply institute its own supervisory training classes or distribute literature addressing the matter. The problem is as much one of cost as it is of attitude. Individual firms must shoulder all the costs of training programs. The most well intentioned employer or supervisor may find little room for this in terms of labor hours or material costs, given the competitive nature of the industry. In many respects, it is the lack of market mechanisms capable of breaking down racial and gender biases that brought on the institutional responses of affirmative action and set-asides.

There is a final consideration in the trends and directions of nontraditional participation in the building industry—the nontraditional employer. Just as individual workers have historically fought uphill battles in securing employment, there have been difficulties for females and minorities at the contracting level as well.

In 1987, the Census of Minority Owned Business Series reported a total of 108,502 minority-owned businesses (U.S. Department of Commerce, Bureau of the Census of Minority Owned Business, 1987). This included 36,763 black-owned, 55,516 Hispanic-run, and 16,222 Asian, Pacific Islander, American Indian, or Alaskan Native–operated firms. The 1992 census showed significant increases in minority ownership (U.S. Department of Commerce, Bureau of the Census, 1992). Firms owned by blacks increased to 43,382. Those owned by Hispanics rose to 97,478, while firms owned by Asians and other minorities moved up to a total of 28,295. The total of 169,155 minority-run construction businesses represented a nearly 57 percent improvement in minority firm ownership over the 1987 totals.*

For comparative purposes, the 1992 Census of Women-Owned Firms showed an increase of 89,387 women-operated construction firms over the 1987 census (U.S. Department of Commerce, Bureau of the Census, 1992). This near doubling of companies stands in sharp contrast to the changes in minority ownership and in female construc-

---

* Although data collection methods changed between the two census surveys, there is no reason to doubt an upward trend. However, the dramatic increase in the Hispanic-owned segment of just over 75 percent could indicate greater efficiency by the Census Bureau in the 1992 count.

tion employment. The women-owned data are not broken down by race, while the minority reports are not differentiated by gender.

Data collection notwithstanding, the fairly strong increases for minorities and women can be viewed in two ways. From a positive perspective, there has been strong growth in the numbers of minority-owned construction firms. This can be attributed to the concept of set-aside awards on public works, special bidding considerations in the private bidding process, and upward mobility within minority groups.

A less optimistic view focuses on payroll and gender. Payroll is important because in 1992 approximately 20 percent of minority-owned firms, or slightly more than 34,000, operated with payrolls. This was 11 percent less than the percentage of all white-run establishments that had employees in 1992. It also compares less favorably to female-owned firms, which had approximately 65,000 shops with payrolls out of a total of 184,000 (35 percent). Again, the statistical information does not delineate by race or sex to the point of accurate comparison, but it does indicate that minority-owned firms have a higher percentage of companies in the competitive or small-shop end of the industry. In part, this can explain why in the 1990s some male minority employers had joined forces with Associated Builders and Contractors (ABC) employers to challenge Davis–Bacon requirements as discriminatory. Yet the evidence also points toward internal market barriers that have stymied capital formation among minority-run construction companies. Generally, public works projects would require that only contractors with employees and certain levels of experience enter the bidding process. The issue of standardized prevailing pay rates needs to be considered with the ability of firms to meet all the requirements of the government body soliciting the work.

There is a historical link between the low levels of minority/female employment and the development of nontraditional business ownership. The early lack of minority work force participation served to limit the dissemination of trade knowledge and the creation of specific construction industry skills. This denied access to a fundamental path of entry into contracting. While modern employers can buy into a shop, early-twentieth-century employers usually had a physical attachment to a trade. The widespread use by municipalities of licensing requirements added a significant roadblock to the creation of minority-run businesses.

Through a series of affirmative action–type programs, government agencies have attempted to encourage minority participation in the management side of the industry. This has entailed the use of bid specifications, set-aside requirements, and the categorizing of disadvantaged employers by the race or gender of the owner.

The creation of minority business enterprise (MBE) and disadvantaged business enterprise (DBE) categories was intended to foster business participation by previously excluded firms. Following the *Croson* decision in the Supreme Court of the United States (1989), cities and states began to reexamine their methods for establishing minority- and gender-oriented programs. The federal government targeted percentages of construction contracts to MBEs and DBEs. In January of 1995, agency heads of federal departments were authorized to use price preferences and set-aside contracts for "socially and economically" disadvantaged firms owners (*ENR,* March 27, 1995, p. 10). Localized programs such as New York City's economic development zones have attempted to tailor efforts to ensure minority firm participation in the local construction economies.

Part of the result was to increase competition between nontraditional groups as such to secure a segment of the work. The dispute focuses on white female–run companies as opposed to minority-operated businesses. As early as 1988, minority business interests claimed that the set-aside work had been awarded to women-owned businesses in a disproportionate manner. They challenged the allotment of set-aside work on Chicago's Dan Ryan Expressway project, which was heavily awarded to women's business enterprises (WBEs). The owners of WBEs responded with overall statistics to show that there was no exceptional treatment (*ENR,* March 24, 1988, pp. 10–11). The situation underscores the competitiveness of the industry and the difficulties of implementing set-aside programs.

The 1995 Supreme Court decision on the *Adarand* case *(Adarand Constructors Inc. v. Peña)* subsequently left many of these minority incentive programs in a state of limbo. The case focused on the manner in which the federal government set aside portions of contracts for the purpose of increasing minority firm participation on government-sponsored jobs. The result of the decision was to create a review process by federal agencies that requires a "strict scrutiny." While it did not bar affirmative action in procurement, it necessitated that such programs must "serve a compelling interest" (Bureau of National Affairs, May 29, 1996, p. 394).

A final trend, which is not as clear in terms of its direction, has been that of confrontational demands by urban minority-group coalitions and community groups. In some cases this has involved picketing and negotiating for entry-level jobs in the semiskilled trades. In others there have been instances of assault, riot, and trespass that have led to indictments and convictions. In New York there were convictions for attempting to shake down builders. While trade journals often report increases in the level of these activities, the future of such occurrences seems to lie with the overall vibrancy of the urban economies.

In 1991 the New York City police department reported 591 contacts involving job-site disruptions—a sharp rise from the previous year (*ENR,* July 12, 1993, p. 8). Urban construction and infrastructure projects are easily targeted by groups seeking employment for community members. There are clearly distinctions among the types of organizations that act to place unemployed workers. The problem arises when specific coalitions physically intimidate existing workers and branch out into extortion.

Although the social composition of the industry has undergone fundamental changes since the 1950s, a more encompassing trend has developed in the structure of the industry. This can be seen in the maturation of the configuration of the twentieth-century construction market. The rapid firm entry into the building market, low capital requirements, and minimal licensing restrictions have historically served to create a competitive market system composed of small units of capital. The Mom-and-Pop shops, the one-person firm, and the itinerant contractor have been commonplace participants since the earliest beginnings of market-based construction.

Yet the development of the construction industry should not be fundamentally different from that of other market industries. The latter part of the twentieth-century seems to provide evidence to support this claim. The early-nineteenth-century artisan manufacturers evolved into the post–Civil War corporations. McCormick Reapers became International Harvester and the pastoral American farmers became the Birdseye corporations of agriculture. So, too, the merging, concentration, and centralization of capital have produced the powerful and dominating construction firm of the late twentieth century.

Construction firms have expanded from covering one specialty area to providing a broad range of construction services. Generally, three categories with distinct market structures have emerged in the latter half of the twentieth century. These include general contractors, general contractors who control their own subcontractors, and a relatively new "supergeneral contractor," which offers the client a one-stop shopping approach to construction needs.

Traditional general contracting has always operated in the following manner: An architect, engineer, or tenant solicits bids for a complete project. General contractors enter into this competitive bidding process. The successful bidder then parcels out the segments of the job to a wide range of specialty contractors. This approach, while the mainstay of private construction, has been altered by the advent of the construction manager, public works legislation, and competition from alternative construction firm structures.

To the largest extent, local firms have continued to operate in the same milieu as their historic predecessors. Firm size grows rapidly in expanding markets as the volume of work increases. As downturns occur, a paring of the work force and movement away from a firm's traditional base markets are seen as logical business decisions.

Despite the fragmented nature of the industry, large, nearly self-contained companies have evolved out of basic primary contractors. Fluor Daniels and Bechtel are good examples of this type of development. Firms such as these often incorporate their own mechanical and masonry trades, thus creating a unified system of control on large-scale projects. Their significant size imposes certain administrative costs, but produces enormous economies of scale. Thus power plants or huge public works projects are often targeted by these self-sufficient prime contractors.

Finally, there is an indication that construction firms are capable of moving beyond the confines of the design-and-build portion of a project. Conceptually, this is the same notion of offering cradle-to-grave care for a prospective customer's building site. The general contractor will not only create the structure but will provide ancillary services, related equipment, and maintenance for the life of the tenancy. A major proponent of this scenario is EMCOR (formerly JWP), which has purchased a variety of building trades contractors, material suppliers maintenance firms, and technology services companies.

Such a novel approach runs against the historic grain of the industry. Here, the hallmarks of successful firms have been flexibility in project requirements, limited overhead, and ability to move in and out of markets. Yet as Peter Cassimatis has noted, the failure to develop vertical integration has consistently served to retard development of the overall construction sector (Cassimatis 1969, p. 123).

CHAPTER 5

Construction Statistics

The construction industry presents somewhat of a statistical quandary. The problem lies in the comparability of inputs and outputs, due to the nature of the industry. Building projects are rarely similar, while virtually identical undertakings are practically nonexistent. Factors from soil type, to weather, to code requirements help ensure that comparability becomes a project unto itself.

The proverbial apples versus oranges issue is for the construction analyst a problem of sheetrock versus plaster, fiber-optic cable versus copper wire, or polyvinyl chloride pipe versus copper tubing. As product development, legal restrictions, and consumer demand change, so does the final outcome of a construction project. Thus the challenge is not merely to develop reasonable weights and measures, but to determine a consistent database for any analysis.

Data collection is itself a hurdle for gaining a statistical understanding of the industry. The difficulty lies at two levels. The first is with collection. Construction statistics are gleaned at the local, state, and federal levels. They are logged by a plethora of agencies, each adopting numbers and codes that are satisfactory to its own statutory requirements. Even at the national level, two important sources of economic data from the Department of Commerce employ two related but different measures of construction activity. The *Survey of Current Business* relies on the gross domestic output contribution as an indicator of construction activity, while the *Construction Review* focuses on the "Value of New Construction Put in Place."

To make matters worse, there are inconsistencies and truncated databases within the departments themselves. The publication of the "Value of New Construction Put in Place" in 1976 (U.S. Department of Commerce, 1976), which resulted in footnotes cautioning against comparability, made post- and pre-1976 data difficult to use in a time-series analysis. In a similar fashion, changes in the standard industrial code (SIC) classifications in 1987 left the *Survey of Current Business* gross domestic product (GDP) series with a time break. The gaps often result from efforts by the data gatherers to improve their statistical counts. Since the published reports are combinations of estimates and raw data, the Commerce Department and the Bureau of Labor Statistics make significant attempts to refine the process, and there are splicing techniques that to some extent can combine the pieces of a series.

Safety figures suffer from a similar tabulation limitation following the Occupational and Safety Health Act of 1970. The legislation improved injury reporting and estimates of hazardous industrial conditions, but data are difficult to compare with pre-OSHA job-related injury categories. In the case of safety information, however, the OSHA standard classifications have been in place long enough to notice trends and changes in various types of occupational illness and injury. Local and state surveys can be even more exasperating, with annual collections becoming biennial or nonexistent following budgetary legislation.

Despite such difficulties, there is still a relatively large body of statistical information available concerning the construction industry. Facts and figures are kept for input materials and prices, structural outputs, wages, and employment. Five-year industry census surveys provide in-depth studies of value-added and industry patterns. For the purposes of this text, a brief survey of the available sources will serve as a good introduction without becoming bogged down in the esoterica of the specific parts of the industry (e.g., terrazzo employment or vitreous fixture production).

There are numerous reliable sources for construction information. The federal level provides two key bodies of data collection through the Department of Commerce and the Bureau of Labor Statistics. States often have their own annual economic reviews containing a variety of industry and employment statistics (e.g., New York state's *Employment Review*).

The Bureau of the Census within the Commerce Department has created the well-known "Value of New Construction Put in Place" series. Since 1915, the series has tabulated public construction actually installed during the stated periods. The "Value of New Construction" is a popular indicator of industry trends, and is inclusive of numerous construction outputs. Actual and estimated data from public and private sector construction projects are combined to create aggregate industry values. A variety of construction market categories permits comparisons and analysis of movements within the industry. As noted by Peter Cassimatis (1969), the "Value of New Construction" series includes force account work, which is the value of work installed without the use of outside contractors. Typically, this involves noncontract construction projects undertaken by large firms and utilities. Thus comparability of data sources based on contract construction hours and wages becomes problematic and must be considered appropriately.

The series also offers values in present and constant dollar amounts. While this is an additional insight into movements within the industry, it presents another serious research issue with respect to the deflator. The numerous choices for deflators and the lack of homogeneity in construction inputs and outputs is a cause for concern when attempting to use real cost and output amounts. The issue is addressed further in this chapter.

As a data source, the *Survey of Current Business* can provide value-added data in its gross product originating (GPO) series. These figures are calculated in current and real terms, as a proportion of the overall GDP, and date back for construction to 1947. The monthly volumes also highlight tables from *Construction Review*.

The Bureau of the Census also produces the annual *County Business Patterns* (*CBP*) survey including detailed information for the entire nation and by county. Census department numbers found in the *CBP* series reflect the total number of employees working for establishments within specific counties. Thus, these cumulative figures indicate the size of firms by number of employees, thereby reflecting industry employment concentration at the SIC four-digit level. This makes it possible to obtain a consistent breakdown of firm sizes by revenue and employment for geographic areas since 1948. The advantages to this survey are its disaggregation and availability over time. The disadvantage for construction industry research is that it lumps both field and support personnel together in its employment data. The series also neglects force account work, but does capture most of the contract construction within its defined areas. The data are tabulated based on the location of firm home offices so that employers counted in one county may actually be responsible for construction projects in another locale.

Construction Industry Census Reports provide detailed information on industry operations by region, state, and specific subdivisions. The census contains expanded coverage on value-added revenues, wages, hours of work, and employment. It distinguishes between supervisory and field employees, which provides insights into productivity changes and technical requirements. The industry census also contains detailed statistics on business receipts, which can be used for an analysis of concentration ratios or movements in firm revenues.

Another aggregated source of construction data is the Bureau of Labor Statistics (BLS) reports on earnings and employment. These yearly reports, which are essentially annualized compilations of the monthly reports, provide solid information on contract construction wages, work hours, and numbers of employees. Hours and earnings are reported for contract construction, general building contractors, heavy construction contractors, and special trades contractors. The same categories and subcategories are used in order to track the number of employees on contractor payrolls.

Construction Review (*CR*), published by the U.S. Department of Commerce, is an important compilation of construction industry data. It features the "Value of New Construction" series, and lists the above-mentioned BLS tables and numerous specialty statistics. The quarterly report includes a multitude of tables on construction put in place, housing, permits, prices, and employment. The importance of *CR* as a statistical resource cannot be overstated. The thoroughness of the compilations and the fact that it is not an industry trade association publication make it an invaluable tool for construction analysis.

While the federal government is a primary data source, there are also a number of useful local public agency reports as well as private publications. States, cities, and counties will publish output and employment reports, although much of the work suffers from redundancy with the *County Business Pattern* surveys. However, specific segments of the industry may be well documented, and statewide movements and patterns are often tracked by state and local labor department agencies.

Privately published accounts are also important sources of construction news and information. McGraw-Hill's *Engineering News-Record* (*ENR*) is a respected weekly publication that provides newsworthy accounts, historical information, and a limited statistical report. McGraw-Hill's *Dodge Reports* provide current status reports of planned and ongoing construction projects. The *Dodge Reports* and similar releases such as *Brown's Construction Reports* are important avenues of information for employers in their quest for bidding opportunities.

The specific information available to the researcher can range from monthly employment data to historical wage and benefit series disaggregated by trade. Employment figures are available for contract construction employers through the Bureau of Labor Statistics. Generally monthly labor reports contain data on employers by industry and trade. Typically, the statistics are national and refer to the numbers found on individual employer payrolls.

Yet despite the numerous statistical sources, economic analysis is confronted with issues of comparability. At the heart of the issue is the nature of the construction industry. Custom made projects create heterogeneous outputs. Unlike the stationary factory with its similar or identical products, the building industry is constantly faced with an assortment of variables. The need to establish a common denominator thus becomes a singularly significant challenge. As Robert J. Gordon noted, it would have been helpful if the federal government "had regularly built sample structures of given types and kept track of their prices" (Gordon 1968, p. 417).

Gordon's tongue-in-cheek suggestion moves to the center of the construction industry statistical question of comparability. The macroeconomist can rely on gross domestic product as a gauge of a nation's wealth in both real and nominal values. The construction analyst is not so fortunate and must be cautioned about the use of deflators. The substitution of consumer price indices with a unique and construction-specific commodity index is not often applicable to the wide range of finished construction projects. A number of entities produce indices; their differences provide the basis for a key area of analysis. That area is construction industry productivity.

Productivity is an issue that many people in the industry have gut feelings about. Employers and developers notice bottom-line changes and gauge movements in labor hours from job to job. Workers consider the time involved in day-to-day operations and become familiarized with changes in technique and practice. Yet an effort to sort out capital investment and its effect on output runs into the not-so-small issue of prices, costs, and inflation. What is the best method to remove the inflationary component from the total current values of construction projects?

A number of researchers have examined the problem. Douglas Dacy (1965) argued in his study of productivity and price trends that productivity in construction was being understated. His contention was that the use of a price deflator or composite cost index neglects any technological advances in the industry. By assuming that "real output is proportional to real materials input," he developed a modified cost index that could account for reductions in labor hours.

One of the interesting aspects of Dacy's article is that he conducted his study from a premise that the common view of backward construction productivity was intuitively wrong. That is, firsthand observations of the post–World War II construction process showed it to be conducted in an efficient manner. What was lacking for Dacy was a means for statistical verification.

An important contribution to this debate came from Robert J. Gordon (1968). He focused on the problem of a representative deflator that could accurately measure real investment in structures. Recognizing that the heterogeneity of construction outputs was the source of the problem, Gordon developed a hybrid deflator from available indices, which included Dacy's. Using what is termed a final price of structures index (FPS), estimates were made of productivity growth and indicated a possible underestimation of construction productivity by as much as 40 percent for the years 1948–65.

In 1981 John E. Cremeans examined what seemed at the time to be a decidedly downward trend in construction productivity. Again, real output measurement became a critical factor. In this case, Cremeans could not conclude that this was simply a problem of the proper deflator (Cremeans 1981, p. 4).* One finding that points research in another direction was related to the capital stock of the industry. Cremeans noted that many researchers had found slow growth in the capital-to-labor ratio, which is a fair measure of an industry's use of technology. He pointed out that data on the apparent deterioration of the industry's capital equipment were masking the fact that much equipment is now leased. Although employers

---

* Cremeans's series is reproduced in chapter 9 in a discussion of construction industry productivity.

and employees were well aware of leasing plans for large pieces of equipment, researchers were failing to include these numbers in their analysis. The statistical obstacle arises in the form of a consistent series to explain capital expenditures and thereby source of productivity change.

A final, brief example is found in Steven Allen's measurement of productivity differentials for union and nonunion workers (Allen 1986). Well aware of the pitfalls in attempting to measure real (deflated) output among heterogeneous products, Allen cleverly devised a basis for comparison among actual installations. Using measures such as square footage installed and the student population per square foot, Allen was able to draw conclusions about productivity characteristics while sidestepping the deflator issue.

The upshot of this discussion is that neither workers nor employers can make claims about the changing state of the industry based on current values of construction installations. Total values of contracts and projects reflect the price movements in inputs. An accurate evaluation, whether for union contract negotiations or for a contractor's bidding needs, will be far more useful if the inflationary component is removed. The deflation process is essentially measuring physical outputs from different years against the prices of a base year. Since construction has such a wide range of physical outputs, it is difficult to create a representative basket of construction goods. An index of price changes for this construction basket could be disproportionately influenced by price movements in steel, concrete, copper, or any one of the many important building materials. Weighted indices and construction-specific indices (e.g., the Federal Highway Administration composite index) attempt to account for this problem, but a trade-specific index to explain just carpentry or masonry work is not readily available.

In much the same way that the macroeconomist seeks to finally settle on what she feels are reasonably acceptable measures, the construction analyst must rely on key determinants of the industry's economic well-being. The "New Construction" series, by virtue of its inclusiveness, acts as a good indicator of construction industry activity. While it relies on survey and sampling techniques in estimating the level of current dollar values, it is more clearly focused and encompassing than a number of other measures. Similarly, gross product originating (GPO) gives an accurate portrayal of the industry's contribution to the overall economy. Despite the deflator issue, GPO captures the aggregate trends in the value added from the contract construction industry. Less encompassing but still helpful are statistics on gross business receipts, trade-specific censuses, and geographic surveys activity, which can be readily integrated into an in-depth review of the industry's performance. The factors that significantly influence movements in these measures will be the continued subject of this text.

CHAPTER 6

Determinants of
Construction Investment

The boom–bust nature of the construction industry is well known to all the participants—investors, employers, and workers. The feast or famine mentality that has historically shaped much of the thinking and planning has largely been determined by the activity in those sectors that demand construction services. As a precursor to an overall economic upswing, rapid construction expansion is often the norm as industries "tool up" for a projected rise in business activity. Its downside is the seemingly instantaneous closing of the investment spigot as overextended construction firms are soon caught with unjustifiable payrolls, inventories, and overhead.

A variety of factors can be identified as contributing to the specific characteristics of investment in this industry. Investment volatility stems from the notion of a derived demand for construction contracts. Decision making in the consumer and investment goods sectors can be combined with the intricacies of the new home-building sector to provide a historical roller coaster ride of immense proportions. In addition, the industry thrives on easy access to construction loans. As the credit markets move, so too will the developers, contractors, and public agencies, along with their construction plans.

To explain cycles in construction, it is also important to consider the products of the industry. A hallmark of the outputs is durability. The structure, the fixtures, and the site are developed with an eye on longevity. Office buildings, homes, apartments, and factories are "built to last" (short-term maintenance and shoddy installations notwithstanding). The endurance of these large capital investments leads to cyclical replacement and repair. Significant portions of these structures, such as roofs and boilers, have, on average, twenty-year life expectancies, which contribute to the periodic flow of capital expenditures.

It is not difficult to produce a scenario in which the structure and durability of the industry's outputs leads producers to misjudge their investment positions. Typically, a large number of small and medium-size builders and contractors gear up for the short term, often as "seat-of-the-pants" businesses that expand investments once a boom is under way but are often too slow to react as an economy moves into a trough.

Historically, home building is an example in which over-building of durable structures prolongs the construction boom. Yet it is the very durability of the final output that postpones the start-up of another boom. As Robert Mathews has noted, the strong labor force attachment of tradespeople and the relatively low capital outlays for firms creates a situation of investment decisions based on an appearance of cheap costs (Mathews 1959, p. 95). Thus the halting of home construction building booms can be a slow process.

An internal market brake for high-rise undertakings is the cost of borrowed funds. Apartment construction projects are notoriously interest-rate sensitive. High-rise dwellings for the middle- and upper-income brackets begin in the same investment environment as single-family homes. However, the costs of a skyward-bound construction project are often backed by floating rate (variable) loans. Portions of the project are loaned at a fixed rate subject to reevaluation over time. As interest rates rise faster than market rental or sales price rates, builders are forced to weigh the costs and benefits of continuing the project. Should marginal interest costs plus existing construction costs be gauged to exceed marginal revenues, then such building sites may be closed despite the fact that the construction phase may be well under way.

The decision for project approval or rejection can be considered in intuitive terms. What is the expected return versus cost of construction at the present rate of interest? Potential investors must feel comfortable that the internal rate of return (the yield from the project) will exceed their minimum acceptable rate of return (Ruegg and Marshall 1990, p. 67). In computing these returns, or in similar cost-benefit types of analysis, the role of the interest rate is critical to the final approval for the project.

This can be contrasted with single-family or attached-housing developments. There are a variety of financing possibilities, but a typical program follows the pattern of "build and sell." In this case, construction takes place in phases. As units are sold, cash is raised to further expand the development. Clearly, demand for the dwellings is affected by a variety of economic conditions. Again, sensitivity to interest rates is crucial in the success of any housing boom.

The role of national income levels is illustrative of this. Economists have long understood the relationship of changes in national income and changes in consumption habits. Housing can be treated as a highly durable consumption good, the demand for which is readily traced through income change and its social aspects.

Classically, from the time of Adam Smith, rising national incomes were associated with rising marriage and birthrates. Smith argued that the development of a nation's population was influenced by the economics of labor market competition. The classical position would argue that an increasing demand for housing would result from periods of prosperity due to an increase in marriages and the expansion of family size.

An additional impetus to housing demand is found in its social determination. Upward mobility over the long term for immigrants and minority-group members also introduces first-time home buyers to the housing market. Shifting social norms during the latter half of the twentieth century have created housing demand by single-parent families, unmarried partners, and single home buyers.

Another important influence is population migration. Demographic flows obviously result in booms and busts for the affected geographic locations. Movements away from one part of the country can leave local builders devastated and the market in a tailspin while having the precise opposite effect on the recipient locale. On the other hand, waves of foreign immigration have the clear influence of rekindling the demand for shelter. The specific extent of this demand change is based on the wealth of the immigrants and the factors propelling their migration. Historically, there have been labor-market demands for different types of immigrants (e.g., 1980s white collar professional immigrants, or nineteenth-century European laborers), which is ultimately translated into demand for some portion of the nation's housing stock.

The significance of this is that a rising demand for housing is initiated through economic expansion in other sectors, which feeds the rise in income. The resultant home-building expansion enters into an already robust economy. Builders with a slow reaction time are at a significant price disadvantage for land, labor, and materials.

The question of time lags in the construction cycle can also be addressed through the use of home building as a proxy. The timing of investments in construction should not be viewed as distinctly different from any other economic sphere. Building homes to capture a perceived rise in housing demand has obvious similarities to the expansion of an automobile manufacturer in an attempt to capture a burgeoning demand for cars.

Home builders have been notorious for their slow reaction to the beginnings of an upswing, and their failure to identify downturns in the same market. Thus, rising unfulfilled demand leads to a rapid price increase at the beginning of a boom, and this attracts additional builders into the market. The time frame for production of housing units inevitably leads to an output of unsalable structures. Completed projects enter an already saturated market, producing the phenomenon of the overbuilt housing industry in a time of weakened demand.

Commercial building markets are not immune to this same situation. Office-building construction, for example, in New York City during the 1980s, mirrored this pattern. This led eventually to relatively high vacancy rates and falling rental prices in the 1990s. The massive scale of high-rise construction establishes a quantitative distinction between construction outputs and most other commodities. The ability to halt a production run, sell off inventory, and temporarily close a facility has no exact counterpart in the construction industry.

Public construction exhibits a similar set of circumstances. Since public goods may not lend themselves to market analysis, the political process can result in a misallocation of market outputs. A good example is the modern infrastructure expenditures and capital improvement in highways, bridges, and tunnels.

Neglected maintenance, heavy usage, and revenue considerations allowed the vast American highway transportation system to seriously decline from the 1960s to the 1990s. Bond issues, tax appropriations, and toll collections were aimed at improving automotive transportation despite the growing sense of urgency about environmental issues, population growth, and overdevelopment. Thus, while federal and city officials debated a reduction of automobile entry into metropolitan areas, suburban communities and local highway authorities were engaged in long-term roadway expansion. The ten-year project on the Brooklyn–Queens Belt System in New York City and the additional lanes for the Long Island Expressway were all forged amid a public debate over fossil fuel usage and special energy taxes.

As a culmination of various market needs, construction takes on a fragmented existence. Since the source of demand is a variety of end users (consumers, government, and commercial enterprises), the building industry lacks a level of self-propulsion associated with other types of investment. Yet there are two considerations that should not be overlooked.

Construction as a $400 billion industry is a significant contributor to gross domestic product. The job-creating capability of a labor-intensive industry is rapid and enormous. The value-added portion of the construction sector is hardly insignificant. As an industry, the builders, architects, engineers, and field employers pump considerable sums of wealth into the wider economy. The economic impact of such output is similar to growth spurts in a number of domestic industries.

Internally, construction output is influenced by technological changes in buildings themselves. Since the beginning of time, improvements in dwelling structures have led to the obsolescence of previous homes. Under the organization of market enterprise, superannuating can lead to a generation of demand for new types of commercial and residential buildings.

For example, the 1995 vacancy rate for commercial office space in downtown Manhattan was 20.2 percent (*Crain's,* July 1996, p. M20). Yet the vacancy rate for buildings constructed from 1980 to 1984 was only 13.4 percent. In fact, commercial space built prior to 1980 had an unweighted average vacancy rate of 23.8 percent. Inadequate wiring for advanced communications, light, and power, as well as energy inefficiencies, made such structures far less desirable than their newly constructed counterparts.

Similarly, in housing, the rise of modern technological advancements provided an incentive for families to vacate older dwellings. Turn-of-the-century novelties such as indoor plumbing and electric light became standard features over the next fifty years. The growing demand for basic conveniences overcame the issue of durability, leaving antiquated structures for renovation or demolition.

As construction moves through its boom–bust cycles, it remains subject to the vagaries of the overall economy. Robert Heilbroner noted that the business cycle appears as a series of crises performing a "curative function" for the general economy (Heilbroner 1978, p. 70). The resulting institutional and structural shifts, as identified by David Gordon, provide a reconstituted economy capable of expansion beyond its present productive state (Heilbroner 1978, note, p. 76). Construction would seemingly be swept up in any output growth or decimated by a rapid decline.

A. Gary Shilling described a set of influences on the construction cycle that encompasses a wide range of macroeconomic markets (Shilling 1988, p. 12). The first, inflation, is a driving force in determining land values and therefore the costs of development. Second is the government, by virtue of its taxing authority. Shilling argues that the 1986 tax reformation reduced many write-offs for real estate development, thus explaining a newfound hesitancy to undertake additional projects. The Federal Reserve Board is his third key influence. Easy money in the early-to-mid-1980s permitted a large volume of leveraged land deals. The subsequent real estate debacle of the late 1980s and early 1990s resulted in an end to this expansion. Finally, Shilling focuses on slowing population growth, which tends to retard growth in the construction industry. The four influences—inflation, taxation, monetary policies, and demographic change—came together to curtail a nearly fifty-year upward expansion of the overall industry.

In a similar fashion, the local construction market follows the movement of the local economy. An example of this caboose type of reaction is underscored by a report from a former adviser to the president of the New York City Council. Stephen Kagan's hypothesized link between taxation and private sector economic activity argues that employment suffers as taxation rises (Kagan 1992). For the particular time periods considered in his study there is a significant reduction in construction employment. It is not difficult to notice the relationship between construction industry activity and the overall state of the local economy.

Clearly, the connection between economic activity and the construction industry appears as somewhat commonsensical. Yet an important final element to construction investment is the concept of the accelerator. By definition, the investment accelerator is the propulsion of a portion of investment by demand. The wide range of possible decisions can make prediction of investment behavior fairly ambiguous. However, there are significant factors that can allow a researcher to maintain a handle on the scope and direction of these investments. For construction, the notion of derived demand adds an additional level of complexity. This must be considered in light of the specific characteristics that shape the industry. Capital stock requirements are seldom balanced by the investment plans of contractors and developers.

This is not to say they are unrelated. It is not difficult to create scenarios in which a number of factors coalesce to cause investment to exceed or underestimate the level of construction demand. As noted earlier, there is a tendency for construction booms to outlive their social and economic usefulness. On the other hand, a slow response to market conditions is a feature of the industry that must be considered in exploring the accelerator.

The uniqueness of construction products suggests that there would be a separate accelerator for each segment of the industry (public, commercial, and residential). Since housing is often used to exemplify the building industry in general, it serves as a useful model in this case as well. Housing units can then be thought of as additions to the nation's capital stock.

Keeping in mind the boom–bust nature of the construction industry, it is important to consider the basis of its instability. It is evident that "a constant population requires no additions to its stock of housing" (Dernburg and McDougall 1976, p. 272). Thus, the demand for new housing is related to growth in population size. Unless there is zero population growth, the potential for housing demand remains positive, provided there is real income growth. This income growth is necessary to fund the demand for additional housing, since unemployed additions to the labor supply cannot stimulate housing demand. It is assumed that capital stock (including housing) will rise only as output rises. Thus, while new housing is linked directly to population growth, it remains a function of changes to the level of output.

However, the question of durability with respect to capital stock cannot be ignored. Housing has historically been one of the world's most durable goods. Since the accelerator principle contends that re-placement output is a source of self-generating growth, durability can retard new investment. Simply stated, an economy with extremely durable capital will tend to remain depressed longer then a similar economy in which capital goods wear out more rapidly. The demand for housing vis-à-vis the demand for all consumer durables (e.g., automobiles or refrigerators) must await an exogenous market stimulus.

Similarly, an alternative accelerator is associated with inventory. Inventory cycles are created because they account for two types of output. The first is that needed to replenish the depleted stock, and the second is the amount required to maintain a stock-to-sales ratio.

Assuming that the marginal propensity to consume (i.e., the portion of disposable income spent on consumption goods) is less than unity, consumption will not lead to constant replacement investment. A small increase in consumer spending should result in a proportionately larger demand for replacement goods plus inventory goods (Dernburg and MacDougall 1976, p. 274). With respect to housing, it is not an issue of inventory to sales in terms of the physical housing units. While government policy may consider an inventory of unsold or unoccupied units desirable, the vagaries of developers' investment decisions make this highly improbable. Rather, the key for inventory investment lies with building materials suppliers who must rely on inventories to keep their sales to builders flowing.

It is fair to claim, then, that an unevenness in construction investment is at the heart of the boom–bust nature of the industry. This chapter has been used to demonstrate and explain the wide range of factors that influence the investment of capital into the building market. The physical characteristics of the building trade, the structure of the market, and the demand for construction products are melded together to create the ebb and flow of capital expenditures. Yet the bottom-line needs of investors should not be seen as unique when compared to other industries. There can be no doubt that the profit motive is as key an element in the investment decision as it would be in any free-market endeavor. It is productivity that in turn plays the crucial role in determining the level and rates of that profitability. Over the next several chapters, it is the issue of productivity that will be examined in detail.

CHAPTER 7

The Role of Government

Ever since there has been government there has been public sector involvement in the building industry. From the time of the Pyramids, with their state-subsidized material costs and crude labor controls, to the modern array of civic projects, the role of the state has become a pervasive one. The infrastructure has historically been the domain of government, from roadways to waterways to subways. As government branched out following the Keynesian revolution of the 1930s, so did its role in the construction sector.

Every aspect of the building trade has become involved with the state at some juncture. Safety, training, hiring, and wage bargaining are each enmeshed within the huge public sector expenditures on construction industry services. With a new construction budget in current (1995) dollars of $125 billion and nearly $143 billion of new construction put in place in 1995, the sheer volume of business makes federal, state, and local budgets a significant factor.

Of equal importance is the statutory and regulatory role that has been created at all levels of government. As a purchaser of construction services from the private sector, government has set up a complete network of regulation and oversight to monitor costs and qualities. Such procedures can be generalized, as in the Davis–Bacon prevailing wage legislation, or be specifically targeted for agency work, such as is found in public school construction.

The state has in many respects also become the ultimate arbiter of union bargaining and organizing. From the inception of the National Labor Relations Act (NLRA), the notion of a forum for dialogue has been a preeminent concern. Good-faith bargaining, time clocks, mediation, and arbitration are some of the influences on the negotiating process. For the construction industry, wage contracts have always been framed by the time constraints of any ongoing projects.

The obvious short-term opportunities for employers and employees make quick conflict resolution an industry necessity. Unlike the individual plant which can be closed indefinitely, moved, operated with nonunion personnel, or struck by frustrated workers, the construction site has another set of influences. It has permanence with respect to the point of production, which simply means there is no threat of a "run-away shop." Yet the construction phase of any edifice is merely a temporary condition that ceases upon the issuance of a certificate of occupancy.

As with the rest of industrial America, the sanctity of the contract has been observed since the 1930s. Contracts contain a rigid establishment of worker protections; the nuances added for the sake of the construction process reflect many of the issues developed elsewhere in this text. Common situs, pre-hire agreements, and double-breasting are terms unique to the building trade arena of labor relations. The long-run institutional effects of trade unionism have served to maintain a strong union/nonunion wage differential as well as to provide the protective structure for millions of building trades workers.

Government, by virtue of its self-interest in promoting a harmonious labor setting, created a framework that set the ground rules for organizing and negotiating. This included the stipulation of time periods for conducting organizing drives, holding elections, and altering contracts. The scope of involvement was expanded in the 1959 Labor-Management Reporting and Disclosure Act (Landrum–Griffith), which required that unions provide the Department of Labor with internal financial data.

Collective bargaining in the construction industry had always taken into account the short duration of building projects. The allowance of pre-hire agreements serves as an exception to the general rule "that the union represent a majority of the employees" (Feldbacker 1990, pp. 142–43). In part, this special allowance catered to the needs of an industry comprised of numerous job sites and employers. As noted by Steven Allen (1994, p. 418), the cost of a 1948 experiment in holding majority representation elections proved "staggering."

The pre-hire exception was tightened up somewhat in the 1987 National Labor Relations Board (NLRB) ruling on *John Deklewa and Sons, Inc.* (282 NLRB 1375). Prior to this ruling, a pre-hire agreement would convert to a regular majority agreement once the union could demonstrate majority representation of the employer's work force. *Deklewa* removed the concept of conversion and left open the right of the employer or covered employees to challenge the union representation through an election.

Such departure from the main body of labor legislation is often seen as a way for the government to balance the legal scales in the industry. The disallowance of job-site economic strike picketing and the prohibitions on certain types of recognition picketing clearly weaken the union position, while the court rulings on "salting" and job targeting have enhanced union activities. The term *salting* refers to an aggressive organizing program of the type conducted by a number of building trades unions since the mid-1980s. As a response to declining membership roles and declining market share, unions began authorizing paid and unpaid members to seek employment with nonunion firms. The notion that a union could legally sprinkle activists within the ranks of open-market shops has been an important topic for unaffiliated employers and members of the Associated Builders and Contractors (ABC). Building trade unions argue that the practice is an innovative organizing tool. Others have argued that "salting" is intended to disrupt nonunion job sites, raising the cost of doing business in addition to organizing these firms (Northrup 1993, p. 470).

Informational picketing under certain conditions remains legal, providing it is not found to be directly aimed at gaining union recognition. For example, a construction union could picket a work site with signs informing the public that a certain trade was being paid a wage below the union's minimum. However, if the pickets made it clear through words or literature that the purpose of the picket line was to induce these low-paid workers to join the union, then the picketing would be illegal.

It is under these generalized legal procedures that the national construction market finds a commonality. Geared toward flexibility, the legal issues are subsumed to the competition within the construction industry. Secondary boycotts and secondary object interpretations are designed to allow projects to move ahead even in the face of an external disagreement. Even the legality of union salting (organizing) was upheld in the 1995 *Town & Country* case based on the ability of organizers to conduct themselves as employees during working hours.

NLRB v. Town & Country Electric, Inc. (1995) was a significant U.S. Supreme Court victory for organized labor's construction unions. It is also an important example of the role that government plays through its administrative, judicial, and legislative branches. The NLRB, through its administration of the National Labor Relations Act (NLRA), had originally found that the electrical contracting firm Town & Country Electric had unfairly refused to hire or consider hiring applicants who were union organizers and union members (*Town & Country Electric, Inc.,* 309, NLRB No. 181, 1992). Town & Country argued that some of the individuals were paid union organizers operating under the International Brotherhood of Electrical Workers' salting program.

The judicial role of the government in this instance came in the form of a review of the labor board's findings. Town & Country, an ABC-affiliated employer, had appealed the NLRB's decision in the U.S. Court of Appeals for the Eighth Circuit. The Appeals Court found for the employer, citing paid union organizers as being other than usual employees. The final determination came from the U.S. Supreme Court, which found that a paid organizer could not be treated any differently from another employee or union member. Essentially, the Court argued that union employees might have other loyalties and interests but that in itself did not distinguish them from any other employee. Thus, the union organizers were protected under the National Labor Relations Act.

The final aspect of government intervention in the industry is through the legislative process. While *Town & Country Electric, Inc.,* hinged on the definition of an employee under the labor law, relief from this decision could come from a change in the law. Prior to the NLRA, union organizing was circumspect because it lacked many legal protections. The federal legislature made the important changes in the rules governing how unions can organize, and Congress has modified this legislation on several occasions. Yet the legislators have not chosen to redefine the characteristics of an employee as they apply to union "salts." This does not mean, however, that open shop–oriented groups could not prevail at some future date in amending the labor relations law.

It was with government recognition of the peculiarities of the construction industry that the organized building trades became institutionalized. Considered as a stabilizing influence through negotiation and membership discipline, the strengths of trade unions have tended to reflect outcomes of the product markets. Thus, membership roles, stabilization, and government involvement have moved in reaction to and presupposition of market demand.

The most significant influence of government is found in its role as a purchaser of construction services. Government building programs can be geared toward specific needs (e.g., roads, courtrooms, and so forth) or they can serve as a basis for expenditures designed to jump start a sluggish economy. In either case, the result is that the government sector acts as the indirect employer of a large volume of construction personnel. Just as investment accelerators for the private sector can move or restrain GDP growth, government capital outlays can influence the direction of macroeconomic activity.

For example, wages earned on government building projects are readily turned into consumption expenditures and savings. As a means of economic stimulus, the government can in a sense kill two birds with the same stone—satisfy its construction needs while promoting economic activity. Of course, the debates about government spending cannot be severed from government-financed construction. Inflation concerns, deficit spending, and resource management are all important considerations dependent on general marketplace conditions. It is reasonable to argue that government can prop up an ailing local economy with building investments yet may run the risk of creating inflationary conditions if the investment occurs in an otherwise booming economy.

Much of this debate centers around the underlying funding for such programs. Outlays for public goods are a function of dollar costs but are also the outcome of political decision making. While tax revenues are often the source for such expenditures, state and local governments will seldom have the budgetary latitude of the federal government.

Local and state governments are more apt to look toward the credit markets for specific project funding. Given the balanced budget constraints of most locales, the convenience of borrowed building is difficult to ignore. The source for such financing can be bonding that is approved by a referendum of the general electorate, or can be part of finance packages that include mandated capital improvements.

Bank loans and similar types of credit arrangement are of considerable concern because of the impact of deficit spending on interest rates. As a political sore point, such financing can be considered inflationary and a squeeze on the supply of private capital. The ultimate reservation is that bond issues inevitably restrict future revenue choices, choking off expansions and producing recessions.

There are indeed two sides to the debate, and it should be clear that construction is part of an integrated system. Thus, expansions in the construction sector (even those spurred on by borrowed money) can result in spillover demand in other sectors. The primacy of the economic pump is not limited to a mechanistic application but is dependent on an evaluation of which elements are sowing GDP growth and macroeconomic activity.

Theoretic support for prevailing wage legislation tends to present higher wages as a buffer to the problem of underconsumption.* Since the government sector is an enormously large purchaser of construction goods and services, wage floors will shore up targeted levels of consumption. Although the pre–Franklin Roosevelt Congress did not marshal widespread government economic intervention, the prevailing wage legislation served as a precursor to the coming New Deal agenda. In the rejection of such legislation, free marketers argue that any legislated wage premium is no more then a subsidy above labor's marginal revenue product. The Davis–Bacon Act came on the heels of the 1929 economic collapse, but it is interesting to note that it was also enacted during Herbert Hoover's Republican administration.

Ostensibly the Davis–Bacon Act was designed to insure government purchases against shoddy or inferior workmanship. By eliminating wage competition, government believed that it was reducing the likelihood that contractors would resort to using less-skilled workers. Arguments to the contrary of this higher-skill theory suggest that union wage premiums are a result of market controls over the labor supply rather than an increased skill differential that is rewarded with higher pay rates.

Many states have also adopted "little Davis–Bacon" acts based on a

---

* Underconsumption refers to the inability of consumers to purchase sufficient quantities of goods and services to keep the economy flowing.

similar regimen of principles. Such local laws reflect wage rates in specific areas, the strengths of the building trade unions, and the degree of quality concerns held by the various legislators. The debate over state-run prevailing wage programs mirrors the national Davis–Bacon issue. Threshold levels that trigger these acts, the costs of data collection, and enforcement are intertwined with arguments over job-specific issues. These range from apprentice-to-journeyperson ratios to the distinction among job titles such as helper, trainee, and apprentice. Yet all these of these concerns can be summarized by the research into the bottom-line arguments about the costs of prevailing rate legislation. Some of the research has been too narrowly defined, but there is a wide enough branch of the literature to get an overview of the economic implications of prevailing wages (see Vincent 1990; East Syracuse Associated Builders and Contractors' chapter report on Project Agreements, *CLR*, April 19, 1995, p. 180).

One of the most comprehensive of these analyses was written by Peter Philips, Garth Mangum, Norm Waitzman, and Anne Yeagle (1995). While funded by Local 3 of the International Union of Operating Engineers, the United Association of Plumbers and Pipe Fitters of Utah, and the AFL-CIO, it presents strong econometric arguments in support of maintaining state and federal prevailing wage laws. Philips et al. basically develop a series of negative conclusions about the estimated public sector dollar savings from repealing both state and federal prevailing rate laws.

Their primary argument focuses on the net result, which is cost savings in expenditures less income and sales tax revenues. For example, at a 3 percent reduction in construction costs, the federal government would "save $346 million in construction costs and the federal budget would lose, on net, $838 million" due to $1.2 billion less in income tax revenues (Philips et al. 1995, pp. 72–73). The secondary implications of a repeal of prevailing rate laws are that it would lead to a severe decline in training programs nationwide and result in as many as 30,000 more building industry injuries per year. The dismal outlook would subsequently slow affirmative action advancement for women and minorities by curtailing apprenticeships and formal training programs.

One of the more objective reviews of the research on the prevailing rate debate can be found in Barry Hirsch and John Addison (1986, chap. 9). They examine arguments about biased data collection, cost inflation, and savings during suspension of the Davis–Bacon Act. The authors balance these arguments with a review by Steven Allen finding that the hidden problem with Davis–Bacon stemmed from "inconsistent application" at the point where union wage rates superseded average wage rates (Allen 1983). Prevailing rate legislation remains an important issue in the public sector, as has been shown not just by the research directed toward it but by the political maneuvering that consistently takes place by both supporters and detractors of these acts.

While such legislation attempts to set wage parameters based on particular local standards, the government on occasion has taken a much more heavy-handed approach. Twice, since the end of the World War II–period Wage Adjustment Board, the government has established a formal procedure for stabilizing the industry, forming committees that focused on limiting wage gains and resolving contract disputes.

The Korean War–era Construction Industry Stabilization Commission (CISC) began in 1951 and was dismantled in 1953. As noted by Daniel Q. Mills (1972a), the CISC of the 1950s had a dampening effect on the percentage increases in construction wages. The commission itself was an offshoot of the War Stabilization Board and had little involvement with dispute resolution.

On the other hand, the 1971 Nixon-era Construction Industry Stabilization Committee (also CISC) was concerned as much with contract settlement as it was with wages. In addition to a review procedure for signed collective bargaining agreements, the 1971 CISC worked through a network of localized craft boards to establish a process for review or recommendation in the case of an impasse. The 1971 committee was created following a give and take between organized labor and the Nixon administration. Following the suspension of the Davis–Bacon Act, the 1971 CISC was formed with the legal power to approve or disapprove provisions of construction industry labor agreements. With the advent of general price controls and the slowing of construction wage growth, this regulatory board was dismantled.

The role of government in the construction industry has been a contradictory one. In part this can be explained by the role government plays as both a purchaser of construction products and an administrator of construction legislation.

Buyers in a market system inherently attempt to secure goods at the lowest possible price. Thus, the sheer volume of government expenditure on construction-related items creates issues as to the public's influence on construction product prices and building workers' wages. This is also balanced by the need to protect the public's investment and to insure that purchases on behalf of the people provide reasonable levels of quality, safety, and durability.

All three of our previously mentioned theoretical positions—mainstream, institutionalist, and radical—attempt to account for this public sector activity. Should government have a role in the establishment of construction market prices and wages? Does government, with its immense budgetary mandates, behave as merely another entrant into the marketplace?

The mainstream market-oriented position would follow the basic premises of our friend Adam Smith. The market itself should decide levels of prices and wages. Smith himself may have been preoccupied with the role of kings and ministers as the greatest spendthrifts in society, but the modern debate still revolves around reining in costs. Free market arguments rely heavily on an unfettered bidding system. Private enterprise construction projects enter into a relatively open market system where the individual or corporate purchasers review the bidding process. Their concerns are typically price and quality, and these for Smith are constrained by the strengths of the market.

Keynesian institutionalists attempt to refute such notions through their claims that the relative importance of the government economic sector weighs heavily on the potential well-being of the general public. Therefore, the significant level of government expenditure on public construction requires a more structured approach. The unique ability of government to stimulate a local economy or unleash a burst of inflationary cost spirals has, since the Great Depression, helped to shape government construction policies. Davis–Bacon, the Occupational Health and Safety Administration (OSHA), and the NLRB framework have also set the parameters for political economic struggles over the role of government.

For radical economists, what may in fact lie at the center of this debate is the parallel controversy over the nature of government itself. While free market traditionalists argue to limited government involvement and institutionalists claim a structural basis to the government's activity, a radical economic argument merges politics with economics. The perspective in this case raises the question of the state's obligations to promoting the general welfare of the citizenry. It is an old but fundamental concern from which the construction industry is hardly exempt. To what extent should the state intervene to guarantee construction industry incomes, working conditions, and methods of public construction? Clearly this becomes a polar opposite to Smithian arguments, but moves the institutionalist legislative framework to a greater degree of social responsibility.

Government has, of course, entered directly into the construction industry in cases of alleged corruption. For example, in 1992 the Justice Department investigated the Laborers International Union of North America (LIUNA) about allegations of an organized-crime connection. A mid-1990s governmental probe of New York City's convention center hiring practices led to the New York City District Council of Carpenters' being placed under emergency supervision by the international carpenters' union body (Bureau of National Affairs, July 3, 1996). The lore of union corruption has over many years mixed fact with fiction. While there have been scandals around the country involving inspection bribery by employers, bid rigging, and union extortion schemes, it is not clear that the industry suffers any greater level of corruption than the rest of modern society. On the one hand, a New York State Task Force on Organized Crime study (1988) found extensive corrupt practices in certain areas of New York City's industry. On the other hand, Richard Freeman and James Medoff (1984, pp. 213–17) argued that the available data did not indicate that illegal practices were something peculiar to a union environment.

The federal government has made extensive use of the Racketeer-Influenced and Corrupt Organizations Act (RICO) to investigate activities in many industries. The exposure of union corruption by the Senate Committee on Improper Practices of Labor and Management (the McClellan Committee) from 1957 to 1959 captured the public's imagination. There is good reason for the disappointment and indignation when a workers' representative is found to have betrayed the trust of the general membership. Yet as Ray Marshall et al. noted twenty years ago, "the problem [corruption] was not, and is not, as serious as the publicity would suggest" (Marshall et al. 1976, p. 114).

These many different points of involvement by government bodies highlight the complex relationship between the public and private sectors. Government involvement is perceived one way from the employer's point of view, another way from the trade union perspective, and yet a third way from the nonindustry view. Regardless of political outcomes, it is certain that government, through both its legislative and its distributive functions, will continue to have a major impact on the building industry.

CHAPTER 8

Productivity

Understanding construction productivity has always represented something of a challenge to both analysts and industry participants. Confounding those who would improve it and those who would study it, construction is a labor-intensive industry with a diverse structure. The focal question is whether or not the industry's characteristics have served to retard productivity improvements in construction technology and installation.

To the uninitiated, a building project presents itself as a quagmire of skill differentiation and hand-tool operations that converge at a unique site. A myriad of special-trades employers then direct these operations. The dichotomy of constraining individual self-interest and inducing social cooperation can appear as a mind-boggling task. Yet every day in tens of thousands of locations, these scenarios are played out with varying degrees of success.

Most striking to any first-time observer of a building site are the multitude of hand-tool procedures. A bevy of busy workers, many with full tool pouches and others with complete toolboxes, is an immediate indication of the complexity of the building process. Each day, a variety of workers regularly apply unique sets of skills to different sets of circumstances. Wrenching, ratcheting, hoisting, screwing, cutting, sawing, and one hundred other "ings" mark the pace and the scope of the project at hand.

It is this specialization, directed by special and general contractors, that at first appears as an obstacle to any standardization of the production process. The resulting control of the field-level installation lies to a large degree with individuals extensively trained in that particular aspect of the job. The absence of the interchangeable worker underscores the differences between construction and manufacturing, thereby setting the stage for a unique struggle over productivity.

The heterogeneity of tasks and a peculiar skill structure of construction work can readily befuddle the novice worker, employer, or economist who attempts to measure output per employee-hour. Estimating the costs and labor time that will be incurred on a project can determine the contractor's financial success on a given undertaking. Small-sized projects have little margin for error while larger ones rely on repetitive installations to lower building costs. Large-scale operations usually include procedures for dealing with unforeseen occurrences (extra work orders, overtime, etc.). Even so, an unexpected physical barrier or delivery delay can prove disastrous to a firm's profit margin. It therefore becomes incumbent upon the owners and supervisors to accurately gauge the levels and directions of their trades' hourly output.

The issue of labor intensity and control of the pace of production is framed by the physical requirements of the installation, regardless of the particular market. In repetitive industrial settings, the trend is to replace human labor with sophisticated robotics. In the automobile industry, spot welders and spray painters have given way to cyberspace replacements. These capital improvements respond to preset computerized programs designed to operate in conjunction with the speed of the belt.

Are such capital-for-labor substitutions technologically possible in the construction industry? The answer is a resounding yes! Are such replacements practical and profitable? The answer is maybe. It is not that technology cannot produce a robotic bricklayer or welder (they already exist). The issue is one of capital costs versus value of output. The use of such equipment raises as many questions as it answers.

There is certainly the question of whether such sophisticated equipment can withstand the rigors of the construction environment at a low enough cost to compete with skilled hand labor. In addition, such equipment would have to conform to the many building codes, design, and safety regulations. The growing threat from a litigious society can only serve to inhibit wary manufacturers and cautious contractors from bringing new products to market.

While none of these issues are sufficient to bar capital substitutions, a more focused alternative effect has been the rise of off-site production. Since the beginning of the postwar era there have been a series of efforts to reduce on-site labor time through the use of factory-type production.

Prefabrication is the leading edge of the off-site movement, although it is often stymied by the dissimilarity of construction project designs. Probably no other aspect of the industry is more illustrative of the problems faced by prefabricated constructors than modular housing. With this type of housing, structures that consist of already built segments are trucked to a site and then pieced together. This method typifies the successes and failures of this kind of prefabrication.

By constructing standard apartment units in a controlled factory environment, a builder partially solves the problem of pace and unforeseen delays. The repetitive nature reduces the need for highly skilled tradespeople, while creating inventories of walls, roofs, and floors. Production in such a controlled setting allows a monitoring of output seldom accomplished at the typical construction site.

There is, of course, a set of physical and social drawbacks to applying such aspects of industrial production to the construction process. These can be categorized as physical plant and the social nature of the workplace. Construction projects are generally unique structures designed for specific uses. The flexibility of on-site production is difficult to reproduce economically in the factory setting. Design changes such as the shifting of a partition, lighting redesign, or the relocating of outlets are routinely handled on location. While design change is certainly possible at the factory level, retrofitting becomes more complex once the prefabricated segment has been shipped.

An important additional consideration is that of construction worker response to prefabrication. Since prefabrication limits the hours of on-site workers, there is a history of traditional opposition to such methods. Both union and nonunion sectors have been slow to accept such change at the level of the individual worker. The organized labor portion of the market is capable of providing legal and institutional challenges to prefabrication. Yet there is little evidence that the organized sector has been any more reluctant to adopt technological change than its nonunion counterpart. In fact, orthodox economic theory would argue that the higher-waged union sector would tend to cause a rise in the capital–labor substitution.

An alternative to prefabricated construction of structures is the preassembly of component parts. The objective here is to reduce on-site building hours by putting together fixtures, motors, duct work, and the like during the manufacturing phase. Thus, a motor-generator set is shipped to the job site with much of the packaged wiring and fitting work completed prior to delivery. On-site tradespersons essentially hook up the power and fuel sources or other end-user parts of the operating system.

Even the prefabrication of components is not without some controversy. The issue is the notion of a de-skilling process. While skilled craftspeople are often trained in all phases of their respective fields, they run the risk of becoming mere installers, akin to factory production employees who pump out interchangeable parts as interchangeable workers. The rapid technological development of polyvinyl chloride (PVC) parts and snap-in fittings are steps in that de-skilling process. Clearly, the trend toward a de-skilled work force can be a source of workplace friction. Since the prospect that a lower-waged installer might eventually replace a higher-paid journeyperson looms as a possibility, there are disincentives for workers' acceptance of new technologies.

Yet it is the issue of workplace hours that is at the crux of the productivity question. The pace of the work assigned (i.e., the time required per installation) becomes a determinant of profitability. For the construction employer, there is a mediated form of control. Because technological control, as in a manufacturing setting, is rarely practiced, there is a reliance on what Richard Edwards (1979) has termed simple and bureaucratic controls (direction by an immediate supervisor that is reinforced by an administrated benefits package). In such cases, the foreman attempts to determine the pace while the attractiveness of the wage/benefit payment makes dismissal an effective threat mechanism.

The pace of work and the efficacy of the capital–labor substitution can also be distinguished by the specificity of the work. General contractors' work involving excavation, framing, forming, and erection has made considerable advances in the use of machinery and innovative building products. Trenching and digging have become increasingly mechanized, while concrete production has been aided by premixing, weather-resistant additives, and reusable forms.

By the same token, the intricacies of the special and mechanical trades are dependent on an amazingly varied set of detailed hand operations. While over time skilled workers develop the abilities to apply these hand movements to any setting, there remains an upper limit to the speed of completion of any given installation. Cutting, threading, soldering, welding, and conduit bending can be marginally improved by automatic equipment, but advances are often stymied by on-site measuring, design changes, and coordination disputes.

To offset stagnant productivity, builders have opted for materials with lower installation factors; where necessary they have sought relief from local building codes. Thus, electricians have moved from a generation of black pipe to galvanized conduit to electrical metallic tubing (EMT) to intermediate conduit (IMC), and then increasingly to armored cable, romex, and plastic pipe (PVC). The plumber likewise has progressed from cast-iron pipes to brass to copper, and finally to plastic. Their fittings have changed from heavy, coarse, threaded connectors and solder to flanged, speedy connectors and snap-on fittings that have become familiar to the repair-minded homeowner.

While these hand-installation methods have left the industry with a legacy of labor-hour intensity, the most noticeable economic shortcoming on the part of the employers has been the failure to create economies of scale. This was noted by Peter Cassimatis in his 1969 treatise on the building industry. Unlike other industrial development, the construction industry has never been able to attain the efficiencies of large-scale production. This comes in spite of the present-day fact that there are more firms with a national and international focus now than at any other time in market-based construction history.

Part of this failure is simply the fact that there are millions of dollars of small-scale alteration and jobbing type projects. These jobs lack the essential features of volume production. There is little repetitive activity, no central site, small and erratic inventories, antiquated business controls.

The more interesting concern is why, then, have economies of scale not developed to any large extent on the biggest projects or within the biggest firms? Cassimatis provides an insight, albeit from the 1960s, that is relevant to the present construction industry. He notes that the traditional relationship between general contractors and specialty subcontractors must be continually renewed from project to project (Cassimatis 1967, p. 68). Whereas manufacturers can enter into long-term agreements with suppliers and their labor force, construction employers find themselves continually reestablishing procedures and flows as they enter into relationships with new sets of subcontractors and their workers.

This lack of long-term partnerships begs the question of integration. Why have firms not been more aggressive at integrating a variety of building operations under one ownership? Several of the largest contracting firms have made the effort, but there is substantial anecdotal information to demonstrate the pitfalls of such endeavors. Brown and Root, Fluor, and Fischbach and Moore readily employ local subcontractors to assure compliance with local codes and practices although they use their internal forces for certain segments of the project.

The EMCOR (formerly JWP) experience remains a good example. Founded as a small local utility (Jamaica Water and Power), the company made a serious bid in the 1980s to become a full-service construction company. It expanded rapidly, purchasing a wide range of specialty contractors and computer technology firms. Such in-house coordination would normally be expected to produce the economies of scale associated with a growing firm. However, a dearth of construction opportunities beginning in the early 1990s underscored the variety of obstacles that even the largest and most integrated of firms must face (Gilpin 1993).

While the mechanics of productivity and many of its trends are readily discernible, measurement is a much less transparent issue. The essential elements of the measurement debate revolve around comparability and consistency. These issues provide little comfort to anyone attempting to measure building trade productivity with any exactitude.

The industry offers a dazzling array of finished products. Galvanized pipe, plastic pipes, vitreous fixtures, lighting fixtures, concrete, and steel are just a few of the elements. The conversion from physical units to dollars for the purpose of comparison raises the question of real price determination. This in turn uncovers the problem of an acceptable price deflator given the multitude of physical products.

A long list of potential data sources and indices adds to the complexity of identifying productivity change. Hours that the Bureau of Labor Statistics records must be reconciled with dollar amounts of output produced by non-BLS reporting firms. In addition, the specific areas of construction often weigh more or less heavily within a given index. The challenge is not merely to identify movement in construction productivity but to search for a justifiably accurate deflator. Such a measurement could then be employed to establish a continuous series of real changes in construction hourly output.

CHAPTER 9

Case Studies and the Union/Nonunion Productivity Question

The swirl of arguments surrounding productivity can cause alarm for builders, developers, and workers. Their wildly differing perspectives are often based on basic statistical assumptions or a series of on-the-job experiences. There are, however, a number of concrete examples of ways in which it is possible to narrow the issues and define trends in construction industry productivity.

In the 1980s Steven Allen published a number of construction studies dealing with the question of productivity. One of the key revelations of his work has been to underscore the variations in productivity for different types of buildings. Using production function estimates, Allen provided insights into the underlying characteristics that shape construction output. His conclusions offer a less than definitive explanation but provide plausible determinants to a complex industrial sector issue.

Allen used Cobb-Douglass production functions to measure the quantitative effects of capital–labor ratios, earnings, firm size, regional influences, unionization, and receipts by sector (Allen 1985, p. 64). The empirical results point toward a long-run structural break in construction output. The period of 1950 to 1968 is one in which productivity rises, only to be pushed downward from 1968 to 1978.

The question of what changed from 1968 to 1978 is one that Allen attempts to answer statistically. Six variables are tested for influences, and Allen claims to identify 41 percent of the observed decline. His possible arguments are worth reviewing, although each must be considered in light of its historical setting.

Capital–labor ratios varied in results depending on the data sources. Using net depreciation, Allen found that a falling capital-to-labor rate was responsible for a 0.9 percent drop in man-hour output. The rising labor intensity found in Allen's American Productivity Center index can be explained in several ways.

It is possible that there is a correlation among labor intensity, labor quality, the percentage of workers that are unionized, and the mix of outputs.* Essentially, Allen lays out a schematic of connected effects on productivity stemming from changes in the types of outputs. Increases in lower-skill installations (e.g., homes) leads to a reduction in union labor. With an absence of union workers who are trained through formal apprenticeships and journeyperson classes, productivity falls. Allen noted that a 7 percent reduction in union labor produced a 0.8 percent drop in construction output.

Similarly, labor quality as a variable is positively correlated with changes in building productivity. Allen uses an index to capture the net effects of age and schooling in explaining a 0.7 percent decline in output in his regression results (Allen 1985, p. 664). While median schooling rose, the quality index fell, implying that this was responsible for a net loss in construction output. It is possible again to consider that the product mix determined the demand for younger, inexperienced workers, ultimately lowering output per worker hour.

To understand construction trends it is important to consider the industry within the context of the larger market economy. Allen provides microinsights that blend together the complex issues facing builders and construction workers.

Local and national trends need to be considered in light of economic changes in the end user's product markets. For example, cost reductions and productivity improvements imposed within a client's market can lead that purchaser of construction services to look for savings in any construction undertaking. While there would not necessarily be any spillover effects from a client's production process to that of a construction firm (e.g., automobile manufacturing is technically distinct from factory construction), cost-conscious firms may require price reductions from subcontractors.

The end result for the construction firm is a search for efficiency

---

* Regional shifts resulted in a rise in productivity, but there were no data on product mix, labor quantity, or percentage of unionized construction workers for the particular region.

that will ultimately focus on productivity. It will not matter in the final instance whether the company is being pressured by a client, competitors, or general trends in the macroeconomy. There cannot be immunity from the pressures of competition even in cases where contractors have had historical relations with a company or appear locked into the work at a certain location.

In an effort to integrate movement in the production levels of specific markets with the macroeconomy, it is useful to look at alternative hypotheses. One notion that proves instructional is that proposed by David M. Gordon (1981). In a quest for the sources of productivity decline in the American economy, Gordon argues that a fundamental breakdown in workplace relations led to breaks in a string of upward productivity growth for the nation as a whole.

Gordon's position is that an implicit trade-off of rising productivity vis-à-vis improving standards of living existed from 1948 to 1968. The capital–labor bargain produced a more or less harmonious institutional environment that was predicated upon contract resolutions. Thus, the institutionalization of collective bargaining allowed for the settlement of disputes in an orderly fashion. Job security and the distribution of wealth were the linchpins to the agreement.

The late 1960s and early 1970s—framed by the Vietnam conflict, extensive government spending, and world oil price shocks—set the stage for a disintegration of the workplace truce. Rampant inflation forced an erosion of the blue collar standard of living, while the stagnating economy unraveled any sense of job security.

In response, idled hours from work stoppages and slowdowns rose as dissatisfaction increased among organized labor portions of the economy. If this scenario is interjected into the construction industry, it is possible to support theory and fact. Sharply rising national construction industry wage levels were fueled by rising demand and a rising cost-of-living index in the 1960s. Wage patterns in the late 1960s were often described as explosive, and culminated in the Nixon-era Construction Industry Stabilization Act.

The combination of leveled wage growth and a rising cost of living resulted in a drop in the standard of living for construction employees. At the same time, price controls increased pressures on company profit margins. With both labor and capital feeling the pinch, collective bargaining began to take on a more adversarial character. Following Gordon's hypothesis, the elements of a labor productivity slowdown

Table 9.1

Construction Industry Productivity Index, 1950–1972

Year	Output per hour (productivity)	Percent change from previous year
1947	72.2	—
1948	76.5	5.9
1949	77.3	1.0
1950	79.7	3.2
1951	78.1	−2.0
1952	78.9	1.0
1953	83.4	5.7
1954	87.9	5.3
1955	87.1	−0.9
1956	86.4	−0.9
1957	89.8	4.0
1958	97.5	8.6
1959	98.3	0.8
1960	103	4.8
1961	106.1	3.0
1962	106.5	0.4
1963	106.8	0.3
1964	108.7	1.8
1965	108.2	−0.5
1966	105.3	−2.7
1967	104.9	−0.3
1968	109.3	4.1
1969	99.1	−9.3
1970	95.8	−3.4
1971	100.8	5.2
1972	100	−0.8
1973	95.5	−4.5
1974	86.5	−9.4
1975	89.6	3.6
1976	95.6	6.7
1977	93.7	−2.0
1978	90.2	−3.8
1979	83.9	−6.9

Source: J.E. Cremeans, *Construction Review,* May–June 1981. Derived from BEA gross product originating data and BLS hours data from establishment survey.

were the result of the "emergence and erosion of a vast internal corporate apparatus of bureaucratic control" (David Gordon 1981, p. 30). The circumstantial evidence can be seen in the measure of construction productivity developed by John Creamens (1981, p. 4), expressed as the construction industry productivity index (see Table 9.1).

The number of positive years (years of rising productivity) before

1968 and the subsequent decline in the post-1968 period lends strong support to Gordon's structural arguments. Similar empirical results can be found in Finkel (1990, Tables A-11 and A-14). While Allen is able to pinpoint several technical causes, the Gordon overview develops a macroeconomic and social context for a construction industry productivity breakdown (see Bowles, Gordon, and Weisskopf 1983).

The upshot of this is to be mindful of the building industry as part of an entire socioeconomic system. While the specific industry characteristics as described by Allen exert strong immediate influences, they occur within a unique mode of production. The social relations prevalent in a narrowly defined market economy can help to shape the forms of competition, productivity, and, eventually, profitability.

Of a less comprehensive nature is a contribution to a productivity series created by Peter Cassimatis (1969). The truncated series employed gross product originating figures from the *Survey of Current Business* and construction worker hours from the Bureau of Labor Statistics. These were extended in my unpublished dissertation (Finkel 1991) and the updated version is found below in the figures that follow.

Figures 9.1 and 9.2 demonstrate, respectively, the trends in real hourly construction worker output, and the percentage changes in this measure of productivity. As I noted earlier in the text, these types of real measures are extremely sensitive to the choice of deflator and the categories of workers. The graphs employ construction worker hours only so that these trends do not account for front office and support personnel contributions. Current dollar values of gross product originating in construction were deflated using a spliced Commerce Department implicit price deflator for construction (formerly the composite construction cost index). While the methodology is clearly not wholly adequate, the intention was to develop a sense of the long-term trends in construction productivity.

The graphs do nothing to refute arguments about previous trends in output per hour. The rising trend in output is consistent with the trend of total industry GDP discussed in chapter 4. The movements in hourly production corroborate the Cremeans survey, and there is a noticeable downward drift from 1968 through 1980 that fits well with Allen's findings (Allen 1985). The final period of 1980 to 1993 appears as somewhat static, with percentage change in output moving in blocks one way or the other.

Thus the opportunities for growth in the construction industry are

Figure 9.1. **Real Construction Worker Hourly Output, 1949–1993**

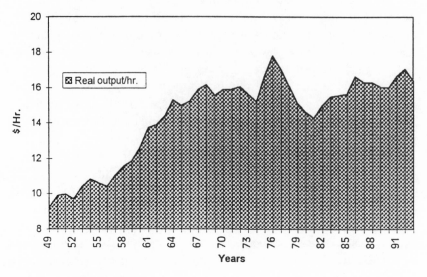

Source: Author's estimates.

Data: U.S. Department of Commerce, *Survey of Current Business;* and Bureau of Labor Statistics.

defined by varied sets of exogenous and endogenous factors. The derived demand of the general economy for plant and facilities is readily tempered by the internal rates of the industry's output. Productivity becomes the ultimate criterion for profitability and, in turn, the key to construction industry investment. Since studies of the peculiar aspects of this industry's productivity are few and far between, the next several pages will review two of these case studies. This assessment will begin to delve into the areas of union and nonunion outputs, the nature of job-site control, and the importance of market structure.

The reliance on historical surveys of the industry to shed light on current productivity debates highlights the problem of incomparability of these various reports. Technical innovations and new types of construction have reshaped the modern world of construction. Yet there are constants in the trades and the mechanics of building a structure that allow us insights into the dynamics of construction procedures. Two examples of scholarly review can provide us with a past and present glimpse into this issue.

Figure 9.2. **Percentage Change in Real Hourly Output, Construction Workers, 1950–1993**

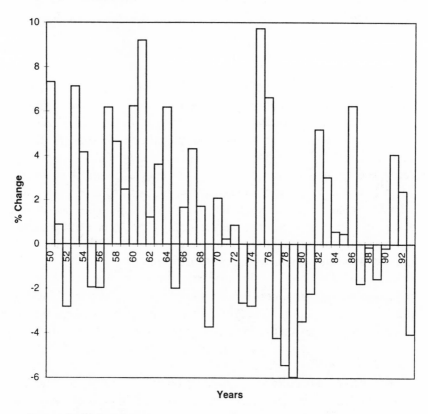

Source: Author's estimates.

Data: U.S. Department of Commerce, *Survey of Current Business;* Bureau of Labor Statistics, *Construction Review.*

The first, by Allan Mandelstamm (1965), is specifically focused on the issues of union versus nonunion contractor outputs in the Bay City/Ann Arbor Michigan areas during the late 1950s. The second is a more general case study by Allen (1986) of the national market distinctions between union and nonunion sectors.

As a focus in an economics text, the narrow union/nonunion debate becomes important for a number of reasons. Union representation has always been a powerful influence in labor relations, work practices, and wages. Even during economic downturns and the loss of member-

ship, construction unions have remained active politically and socially. Union market share often pertains to particular industries or
types of construction. Thus it is important to get a sense of the ways
in which organized workers can and cannot influence the construction process.

Mandelstamm's research followed a classic presentation of the construction industry labor relations by William Haber and Harold Levinson (1956). Mandelstamm's goal was to provide some quantitative
measurement for the issues raised by Haber and Levinson and thereby
move in directions that had largely been ignored by earlier work. His
comparison relied on interviews, estimates, and contractual data with
respect to residential housing markets in Bay City and Ann Arbor,
Michigan. The large proportion of unionized construction workers in
Ann Arbor led Mandelstamm to use this area as a union job proxy. The
relatively light amount of organization in Bay City (40 percent) provided
the basis for a nonunion proxy. There was also a statistical profile developed of union and nonunion employers in the Bay City area.

The overall findings of this research were in essence favorable to
many traditional pro-union arguments. The estimated work hours of
unionized labor employed by Ann Arbor contractors were consistently
lower than those of their Bay City counterparts. Total estimated median hours for the unionized Ann Arbor workers were lower than the
Bay City estimates by over 200 hours.

In a detailed breakdown of union and nonunion trades for the Bay
City area, the number of median labor hours for union employers was
lower for 11 out of 13 trades. The sum of union median hours was 20
percent lower than the like sum of nonunion hour estimates. The surveys also indicated that while total median union wage bills were
slightly higher between the two areas and 11 percent higher within the
Bay City categories, this had little impact on price differential. Ann
Arbor estimates were 3 percent greater than Bay City estimates on
12,500-dollar homes, while nonunion median prices exceeded union
medians by a 7 percent margin.

In interpreting these results, Mandelstamm reviewed many of the
arguments used to distinguish union from nonunion job activity. He
could find scant evidence of technological restrictions by unions, with
the exception of instances such as the Ram Set powder-actuated tools,
which required specialized handling. Typically anti-union arguments
claim that collective bargaining agreements limit technical progress in

a self-serving effort to preserve job opportunities. Mandelstamm found that unions made only the weakest effort to limit mechanization (e.g., there was restricted use of painter's spray guns, which were limited to unbrushable surfaces), while pre-fabrication opposition had already been found to be a Taft–Hartley secondary boycott violation (Mandelstamm 1965, pp. 508–509).

Work rules also had little or no impact on employer stability and the ability to successfully compete with nonunion firms. Claims of output limits, slowdowns, and unusual quality requirements were found to be baseless. While minor jurisdictional issues arose, these and the often-raised claim of featherbedding did little to impede the union employer's entry into the residential market. More importantly, Mandelstamm reported that there was little union interference with hiring and firing procedures.

The study also considered the effects of the means of payment on productivity. By preventing the use of piece rates and lumping (lump-sum payments rather than hourly wages), unions tend to reduce competition between workers. Does the reduction of this competition reduce output per hour? In this particular study there was some limited evidence that lumping and piece work actually reduced efficiency as measured by employee hours (Mandelstamm, p. 512). While the function of a union is to standardize hourly pay scales, the most common form of union merit pay was (and probably still is) overscale wages to key employees.

Three other areas of discussion also provide historical evidence for some present-day issues. The use of higher-waged labor by union contractors requires them to employ their resources more efficiently. The Michigan cities comparison found little evidence of capital–labor substitution and pointed toward the use of more productive workers. This, of course, mirrors the economic logic of workers producing, at the minimum, their marginal revenue product, and questions the value of capital replacement in the late 1950s.

Possible sources for a production differential can be seen in both training and management. The 1957 survey and interviews used in Mandelstamm's research paper revealed extensive apprenticeships, which helped to create skilled journeypersons in a shorter period of time than with the nonapprenticed worker. Mandelstamm noted that "it is not necessarily true that a group of well-rounded journeymen will work with greater efficiency or skill than men less formally trained" (1965, p. 517). What is more plausible is that there is a learning curve for the more highly skilled trades and that formally trained jour-neypersons enjoy a significant income time-horizon advantage over informally trained workers.

Since these better-trained workers move on to command higher rates of pay and superior lifetime earnings over their nonunion coun-terparts, there exist strong economic incentives for union employers to become more cost-conscious. Job planning, material cost controls, and market strategies become essential contractor office tools. On the job site itself there is a need for more efficient levels of supervision and direct control over the higher-priced workers.

Clearly, the Mandelstamm study is dated and focuses specifically on residential housing. Yet many large metropolitan areas have features in their construction markets that have much in common with the subject of this survey. New York City, for example, has a variety of projects in which union employers compete with nonunion employers.

To a large extent, New York City's new high-rise construction re-mains the province of the organized building trades employers, and prevailing rate (government-sponsored) jobs tend to level the bidding process. Yet there are millions of hours in private commercial alter-ations and small residential projects that reflect the conditions found by Mandelstamm in Michigan nearly forty years ago.

An equally illustrative case study is provided by Allen (1986). In his research, Allen enters the debate over union productivity levels by analyzing commercial and school projects in the early 1970s. Using a data sample of eighty-three commercial projects (1973–1974) and sixty-eight school buildings, Allen was able to provide measurements in physical units (e.g., square footage) as opposed to the value-added measures of earlier studies. The advantage to this method is that it avoids the long-standing construction issue of real price deflators. As noted in chapter 5, the extensive use of construction inputs and the choice of price indices can significantly influence real output results. However, while the use of physical measures avoids the deflator prob-lem, it raises several question about the traditional noncomparability of individual construction projects.

Allen argues that there is ample economic theoretical support for a union productivity advantage. He attempts to isolate union influences from those that are price theoretic, such as improved screening and the substitution of "other inputs for labor in the production process"

(p. 189). Institutional union effects such as apprenticeship and hiring halls are seen as positive productivity influences. On the opposite side are restrictive work rules and jurisdictional divisions, which are viewed as impediments to the employer's control over the job-site operations. An indirect effect is considered to be management behavior. In this effect, the employer responds to wage increases through "material management, quality control, cost estimating, or work scheduling" (p. 189).

With this perspective, Allen then develops an empirical model based on a Cobb–Douglass production function, $Q^a = AK^b, L,$ where Q is output measured in physical units. The equation is manipulated to allow for either labor or capital influences as well as the elasticity of productivity with respect to labor quality.

Output was then regressed on capital inputs, capital equipment expenditure, labor inputs (on-site production hours), and a labor quality index of predicted annual income by occupation. Building characteristics were also included through control dummies.

The empirical results for commercial office building proved interesting and led to a strong understanding of the union effects on the construction industry. Regressions were run using both value added per hour and square foot per hour as dependent variables, respectively. As Allen notes, there was 37.6 percent more square footage built per hour on union jobs. The positive union influence is also found when building characteristics are added and when the sample is divided by square-foot size.

In terms of the economics of the industry, the task is to account for this empirical result, both theoretically and practically. Allen cites the union advantages of training, supervisory needs, hiring costs, and management techniques. However, his econometric specification, while supporting a union advantage, is not clear in terms of the source of the differential. Labor quality proxies for supervisory and semiskilled hours reduced the union effect although the explanation of this influence is open to speculation.

Allen conducted a similar study for school construction and the results help to emphasize the importance of market structure in construction. In this case, the statistical evidence pointed toward a larger positive union effect on productivity for secondary schools than elementary schools. The dependent variables used were value added per hour, square foot per hour, and student capacity per hour. The novel treatment of output through the use of physical units could neither pinpoint an industrywide differential nor reject the hypothesis that such a differential exists in school construction.

The upshot of Allen's research is that there appears to be an observable union productivity advantage in commercial construction, while school construction is less clearly differentiated. Allen also tested for the effects of contractor specialization, building design, and the heterogeneity of school projects. Logically, the advantage enjoyed by union commercial contractors should carry into public sector construction but this could not be demonstrated on all forms of school construction. Several possible explanations for the union differentials in commercial and public construction are inherent in the nature and process of public school construction. One suggestion is that government construction projects offer far less flexibility in "material and techniques" than is found in the private sector. State and local authorities are often restricted by the bureaucratic process that develops these projects in terms of design and scheduling. Thus, the flexibility noted by both Mandelstamm and Allen for private building success would be much less present in the public sector.

The use of prevailing wage laws also tends to equalize union/nonunion work forces. Since prevailing rates and helper apprentice requirements reduce the nonunion pay advantage, they would be expected to narrow any union productivity advantages. This explanation relies on a price theoretic effect in which nonunion employers would respond to the higher pay rates by employing their most productive workers.

A noteworthy account for the role of government bureaucracy in the results is related to public sector efficiency. It could be argued that union employers would have a neutral response to prevailing rates since prevailing rates are similar to union pay rates. However, Allen points out that public sector agencies are not compelled to cut costs as carefully as private sector managers. Union employers may take advantage of this fact by using their less productive employees on these sites, thereby allowing union workers to receive economic rents in the form of on-the-job leisure or lower work effort.

Both case studies argue for a positive union productivity influence, but there are also numerous nonunion employers, known loosely as open-shop employers, who are participants in associations that claim equivalent output levels. The next chapter will identify the characteristics of these open shops and discuss how they differ from closed or union shops.

Productivity is a central element to economic growth and essential to attracting construction investment. Are declines in productivity actually caused by shifts in the types of construction and therefore the types of employers? Is an increase in the number of nonunion projects a source of this output-per-hour reduction? The comparison between open and union shops will further help to evaluate these questions.

CHAPTER 10

Competition and Workplace Control

The spur that moves the horse, or in this case the construction industry, is competition. The highly competitive nature of the industry is best understood through an awareness of firm size, capital requirements, and ease of market entry. Economic theorists have devoted long treatises to the notions of competition. With logical and historical justification, economists from Adam Smith to Robert Lucas have provided an abundance of practical competitive models. The prices of any family of goods, the ebb and flow of the wages for a particular skill, and the commonsensical realities of market mechanisms make clear the reality of competitive forces.

The key to applying such concepts to the construction industry lies in establishing a clear perspective of the forms of this competition. It is from these forms that the structure and relations within the firms and the industry become apparent. As a starting point, suffice it to say that we are faced with an industry composed of varying sized units of capital. Each employs waged labor and is bounded by loose arrangements of market rules.

At the center of these issues lies the firm's quest for profits. The explanations by Ronald Coase (1937) of the firm's evolution become ever clearer in the case of construction. The firm, even at its smallest levels, is a more efficient unit of production than the artisan or the independent contractor. The search for work, the question of liability, and the ability to negotiate payment are essential to a smoothly flowing market system. The construction firm assumed these responsibilities during the nineteenth-century development of market-based construction.

The construction firm's ability to generate profits out of its economic activity provides a basis for further investment. The level of these investments represents the cutting edge of the firm's advantage over the independent draftsperson. The increasing size, scale, and pace of the construction industry has been made possible by an industry structure that can satisfy growing levels of product demand. Conversely, only those firms that are successful low-cost producers are able to remain as active agents within the construction industry.

At the small-firm level of the construction industry, output is produced by fast-paced firms with thin profit margins. Employers serve a variety of functions and often work as installers themselves. This is but a step beyond the artisan/draftsperson type of shop, although a small firm can avail itself of many of the legal and economic benefits of the modern firm.

The pivotal elements of small-shop competition are individual skill and on-site supervisory control. Since the small shop is engaged in jobs of limited size and duration, the margins of error are indeed small. Field employees are either equipped with knowledge and ability through general training, or they have become adept at particular repetitive functions. Supervisory control is a critical aspect in terms of marginal error, but clear direction and proper layout are two important components of any smoothly run project.

Market constraints require that speed and accuracy be continually challenged with respect to profitability. Demanders at this level are often residential clients or small-scale commercial enterprises. The ability to pay should be considered because the market price for such projects must reflect the financial position of the buyers of construction services. The low-cost producer is constantly challenged by both reorganized means of production employing cheaper forms of labor (e.g., helpers or general labor) and increasingly productive journeypersons.

This last form of competition, the employment of increasingly productive units of labor, is probably the most important. Skill level can be enhanced in a variety of ways. Efficiency can be obtained through the use of technologically advanced hand and power tools. This is similar to the augmenting of factory production with machine tools at various stages of industrial expansion. Economic efficiencies can also be obtained through technological development in the area of materials and final goods. Lightweight building materials and ease of installation add to the rising output per worker. A final consideration is the overall training level for the general work force. Rising literacy rates and years of schooling would logically be thought to yield improvements in the skill levels of building tradespersons. However, recent periods of declining productivity call such traditional notions into question.

The heart of the production process is the construction site itself. It is here that the engine of the firm cranks out the final product that is in a sense brought to market. The methods of ensuring that output is produced in a timely fashion vary to some degree from firm to firm. This variation can be as much a function of the internal characteristics of the company as it is related to the issue of unions and merit-based shops. By applying each of our three original economic theoretical positions (see chapter 2), it is possible to grasp the essential economic distinctions between these forms of competition. This will provide a basis to understanding the means by which firms and workers compete in the modern-day construction environment.

There is no doubt that we owe a debt to the classical arguments of Adam Smith in explaining the features of competition. Smith realized the advantages of the division of labor not merely in terms of rising capital output but in terms of workplace control. Specialization both by trade and within trades has resulted in a rationalization of the labor process that has roots in the origins of capitalist enterprise. Productivity is enhanced by tried and true structural divisions that have tended to become anchored in historic traditions. For example, the hierarchical structure of control from employer to superintendent to general foreman to deputy and so on has a history dating back to rudimentary market-based construction.

The control process thus has a double-sided focus. First and foremost is productivity. Hourly output is enhanced by skillful supervisors who make efficient use of their work crews. The span of control (i.e., the ratio of supervisory personnel to production workers) is an important aspect of any industrial process. In the construction industry, the span varies with the skillfulness of the tradespeople and the degree of difficulty associated with the installation. Home building, with its repetitive operations and standardized layouts, uses a wider span than complex commercial installations, which can be as narrow as one foreman for every three production workers.

Some unions negotiate spans of control into their contracts. Minimum ratios protect employees by insisting that the employers designate and compensate one of the workers to handle job-site direction and coordination. Maximum spans protect supervisors by limiting the number of workers for which the supervisor is responsible.

The second focus has to do with control over the workplace. Manufacturing processes have long histories of capital substitution, employee assignment changes, and management re-engineering in an effort to reduce unit labor costs. Construction, because of its heterogeneity and hand-tool operations, is less susceptible to such experimentation. Thus, the de-skilling process analyzed by Harry Braverman (1974), and others, is a much more cumbersome innovation when tied to construction. Yet, as Stephen Marglin (1974) and Katherine Stone (1974) have noted, the division of labor serves as a fragmenting procedure that can at times pit trade against trade or limit worker control over the pace of production. Of course, the flip side of such division is the competition among firms that are the beneficiaries of successful jurisdictional challenges (union) or multicraft job assignments (open shop).

Thus, the distinction between open-shop and union construction sites illustrates a central argument over the issue of flexibility. Proponents of open-shop construction have argued that rigidly established divisions of labor retard rather than improve productivity. The argument stresses the need to reduce downtime (leisure rents and nonproductive labor) by providing work assignments that cross trade lines. Obvious examples are the open-shop use of laborers to move materials for skilled trades, or the employment of generalized helpers who can float among different types of skilled journeypersons.

The rebuttal presented by the organized building trades is that such a Smithian division provides productivity benefits that exceed the losses caused by craft jurisdictions. Advantages are produced through formal apprenticeships, hiring halls, referrals, labor discipline, and higher skill levels developed by specialization. The dexterity and knowledge gained through repetitive skill-specific operations serve to increase the individual's physical outputs. In the same way, defined lines of responsibility produce a more harmonious work site in terms of subcontractor relations and employee attitudes.

A second approach is to view the construction site from an institutional perspective. Thus, the large-volume projects are handled by relatively large corporations with their own unique work practices and historical developments. For example, BE&K, the large open-shop firm based in Alabama, was able to establish its own income guarantees; in the opposite vein, unionized firms might adhere to work-sharing plans or job termination requirements.

The institutional explanation for market competition must also account for the entire legal framework that loosely governs the building industry. National codes and safety standards become the minimum requirements that are often the starting point of bureaucratic oversight in the industry. Occupational Safety and Health Administration (OSHA) rules, compensation laws, prevailing rate, tax abatement, and a host of other legalities can alter the scope and direction of a job.

In the most general sense, the construction industry, in its macro-economic role and its significant contributions to gross domestic product, establishes a basis for the interest of local, state, and federal authorities. Specifically, this can be seen in public works jobs, which attach prevailing rate guidelines and distinct building standards. More generally, it is seen in legislated programs such as compensation, disability insurance, social security, and unemployment insurance payments.

The same institutional framework offers a second means to compare open- and union-shop construction. Unionized firms pay their workers based on hourly scales, which have been negotiated through collective bargaining agreements. The structure of journeyperson and apprentice pay usually has a local historical determination, and the pay pacts normally run for one to three years. Defined benefit packages, work rules, hiring practices, and jurisdictional issues are usually found in the working agreement. The effect is to provide the employee with the security of the specific labor exchange as stated in the contract while providing the employers with a time horizon on which to base business decisions.

Open shops are under no such binding generalized constraints with their employees. Under the system of merit pay, employers are able to set hourly rates based on specific market requirements and their own determination of the worker's output potential. The wage bargain then turns into a collection of individual agreements rather than a single collective contract.

The benefit structures of open-shop firms have a wide and varied range, often dictated by the contractor's markets and areas of special-ization. Benefits can range from statutory requirements to limited health and welfare, or can mirror some union packages. The variation across these firms can change dramatically, as noted by Clinton Bour-don and Raymond Levitt (1980) in their study of open-market con-struction companies.

In the unionized sector, the institutionalization of job descriptions, advancement, and supervisory practices is seen as a means to establish workplace stability. Each day the employee and employer have a clear sense of the parameters for the production process. In contrast, the open shop and its supporting associations argue that flexible work structures allow open shops to respond to short-term project requirements and changes requested by end users. The issue of flexibility is of considerable importance in a project that may last for no more than seventeen to eighteen months. Both union and nonunion employers have argued that it is crucial to job management that there be a method of satisfying the immediate needs for design and making emergency changes.

The difference between these two sectors of the same industry can best be seen in the way they are treated under the labor legislation pertaining to the construction industry. Clearly, the National Labor Relations Act (the Wagner Act) established the right of workers to bargain collectively with their employers. The federal legislature has gone to great lengths to develop a framework of conduct within the construction industry (see chapter 7). For example, organizing is permissible under the basic sections of the NLRA, and pre-hire agreements have been upheld under certain conditions. However, common situs specifically bans union picketing at the place of output (job site) during an economic strike. Striking building trades workers cannot interfere with other trades at a common site (construction job) because these other trades are employed by "neutral" employers (i.e., firms not employing striking workers). The common situs prohibition and Section 14(b), which establishes the right-to-work state, have been in place since the 1947 labor amendments (Taft–Hartley).

A final version of the workings of the construction industry markets can be found in the radical economic paradigm. This view can prove enlightening because the industry has a well-publicized, if not somewhat mythical, history of frictional workplace relations. The starting premise is that building trades workers exhibit a fair amount of control over the day's output level by virtue of their manual and cognitive skills. In the course of competitive bidding, wage costs become a crucial factor. If hourly wages and benefits cannot be reduced, then output must be increased. However, unlike the factory where capital–labor substitution is commonplace, the skilled and semiskilled tradesperson has certain irreplaceable abilities. This sets the stage for a struggle ranging from individual soldiering to institutional confrontation.

The nature of the construction industry requires that the employer put a fair amount of trust in his or her employees. Willingness by both parties to adhere to the wage bargain becomes critical. A small employer may at the very minimum entrust the hired tradesperson with significant amounts of the firm's valuable capital. It is common for an employer to hire a new employee who has had no prior relationship with the company. After filling out the requisite tax forms and payroll information, this new hire may be put in charge of a panel truck filled with material and a limited number of tools. In the jobbing sector, much of this occurs routinely with minimal supervision. It becomes a management obligation to provide both direction and detection in order to effectively monitor the employee's performance.

Such monitoring of the labor effort is not without cost. The simplest form of entrepreneurial control is the standard foreman–worker relationship. Here, the foreman, working along with the crew, directly oversees the minute details of each daily operation. The same can be said for the nonworking "straw boss" or subforeman. With higher-skilled labor, the spans of control (supervisory workers to production workers) can fall sharply, which introduces the issue of direction. The problem of detection is another matter. Construction logistics, the heterogeneity of the tasks, and the many miscellaneous obstacles facing workers and employers produce only the roughest of benchmarks by which to gauge performance.

Samuel Bowles (1981, p. 5) argues that the issue of detection grows out of the question of why the amount of output is unspecified in the labor contract. He answers that "the cost of determining and enforcing a contract for a specific amount of work done is in most cases high enough to militate against its use." The simple control over the construction workplace can also be seen in this same context. Employers can hire costly supervision for the purpose of surveillance, or they can opt to pay a wage premium to increase the cost to workers of a job loss.

In the open shop, such choices can be determined by the levels of competitive market pressures. Without a formal wage structure, merit pay must be pegged to each worker's expected or observed output. This in turn leads to a workplace composed of a variety of combinations of satisfied and dissatisfied workers and employers. Dissatisfied workers will attempt to reduce their labor effort while dissatisfied employers will attempt to coerce additional effort. For open-shop contractors, the process of detection and surveillance amounts to an additional cost of operation.

In the union shop agreement, the collective wage bargain applies unilaterally. Categories and their respective rates are established for foremen, journeypersons, helpers, and apprentices with a general understanding among all employees. The variations are small and disagreements as to the intensity of the labor effort range from disputes over implied output quotas (arbitrary amounts) to rewards for above-average performance (over-the-scale pay). The role of the union is to smooth over the area of employee–employer relations by establishing acceptable pay rates, training programs, and referrals. In addition, the union wage premium establishes practices that are seen as reducing the need for costly supervision and the machinery of on-site monitoring. In the end, union labor structures need to be able to justify higher wages through equivalent marginal revenue products without the additional costs of close direct supervision.

The issue of control is ultimately a central concern in the management of any job. Construction firms have had little innovation in terms of management. They rely primarily on a mixture of what Richard Edwards (1979) has termed simple, technical, and bureaucratic control structures.

Simple controls employing direct supervision are the most common form of job-site management. The worker's day begins at the shop or at the job-site locker or point of assembly. The orders of the day are issued by the employer or the foreman, and workers either travel to the jobbing locations or take their positions at the construction site. Supervisors might pass the work areas to review operations, remain on the floor with a crew, or visit jobbing sites. This system for monitoring output tends to be arbitrary and ad hoc, leaving an obvious opening for inefficiencies.

Technical controls are more limited in construction due to the hands-on nature of the operation. In contrast, factories can change their process and equipment, which can determine a worker's mobility, downtime, and individual decision making. The physical layout of the production gang and the pace of machine-induced output is virtually predetermined.

In the building trades there is a vast need for skilled, innovative thinking even in the roughing-in stages of a project. Building design is seldom created with an eye toward physical control of building personnel, while the pace of the job is rarely set by the installation process itself.

Of course, many of the "wet" trades are limited in the range and scope of their activity by the materials used (mortars, plasters, and so forth) and the location of their work. For example, the bricklayer's scaffold becomes a virtual home during work hours and the pouring of concrete involves a race against time to complete the pour before it sets. Yet for the most part, control over heterogeneous work activities by machine process has evaded the building trades.

An assessment of many unionized operations and some nonunion ones finds that labor's cooperation is enticed through a system of bureaucratic control. In these cases, a formal structure of hourly pay and benefits is linked to upward mobility and potential work opportunities. Vested pensions, benefit eligibility requirements, and wage grades become incentives for labor market attachment and increased labor effort. Entry-level apprenticeships, training programs, and secondary/primary market distinctions serve as rungs on the job ladder, ensuring labor satisfaction as well as an orderly advancement for employees.

The mixed bag of controls present in the construction industry reflects the large variation in size and extent of operation of construction firms. In many smaller shops, which are family-run, simple control, where a foreman directly oversees the worker, plays a much stronger role than any other means of workplace discipline. Clearly the need for individual contact, the thinness of profit margins, and the lack of a wage premium form the basis for reliance on first-hand direction and supervision.

The larger job sites create the need and conditions for additional methods of control. The volume of work, the cost of narrow spans of control, and relatively wider profit margins necessitate simple control tactics, to be augmented by bureaucratic structures so as to maintain labor stability.

A developing area of interest from a company perspective is that of project management. While subcontractors and general contractors employ individuals as project managers, the science of project management has been undergoing considerable change. The evolution started with end users hiring construction managers to review the construction phase and to make cost-saving proposals during actual installations.

In an effort to improve bottom lines, engineers, designers, architects, and managers have developed several formats for ensuring job quality. Value engineering was an early foray into the world of cost saving and efficiency. Subjecting plans and specifications to an early review was intended to prevent costly errors and impractical designs. Applying similar concepts to works in progress, general contractors created a number of formats for marketing their firms as construction managers (CM). In some cases, the management service is sold in its pure form. In this practice, firms oversee the existing general and subcontractors for a specific fee. To make such job-site controls worthwhile, the CM must find savings that justify the managers' fees or provide the end user with a certain comfort level about time and quality.

In a variation on this theme, some construction managers hold a financial stake in the building project. These "at-risk" CMs then have an additional incentive for the cost savings that can be found in any construction investment. There are also hybrid CM structures that cross between at-risk construction management and fee-based operations.

Finally, there is total quality management (TQM). This innovative management tool has fit well with cost-conscious firms responding to competitive pressures of the late-twentieth-century worldwide economy. As described by Mills (1996, pp. 114–22), quality management requires a commitment at all levels of the firm. Only through a strict adherence to a measured degree of quality in design, delivery, and installation can construction companies cut costs and schedule time. TQM has clear benefits in that it sets extremely low tolerance levels for errors at all phases of the project. Combining many of the aspects of construction management and value engineering, the practice has been increasingly used on large-scale projects.

Yet typical of the slow historical pace of construction industry change, construction firms have been reluctant to follow the leads of other industrial sectors (*Engineering News-Record,* May 15, 1995, p. 24). Such programs are often expensive to maintain and may never prove cost-effective for small generals and subs. The search for a successful management style is one that has troubled all industries since the time that Adam Smith first noticed the advantages to the division of labor. Just as a firm loses its competitive edge when its management methods become commonplace, so too are some construction companies looking to augment even TQM. Quinn Mills suggests the creation of a system of goals, empowerment, and measurement, or, as he terms it, "GEM" (1996, p. 127). In this method, middle-level supervisors are given leeway to reach targeted project results without the traditional top–down management control.

Clearly, job sites do not run themselves. The need for supervision in the modern workplace is too obvious to be noteworthy. What I have tried to explain in this chapter is the means by which control and direction are undertaken in the construction workplace. The creation of a division of labor and the complex labor institutions within the industry are not historical accidents. They have been rooted in the relationships of the building trades since the master–journeyman arrangement evolved into the contracting system. With this evolution came a progression of management formats. Traditional, simple means of direction are augmented by complex institutional structures of defined benefit plans and workplace rules. These methods, over the long haul, have played an important role in the value-creating abilities of the construction industry. It is in the division of this value, in the form of wages, profit, interest, and rents, that establishes the parameters for stable labor relations and a basis for future investment.

CHAPTER 11

The Determination of Wages

Wage changes for construction workers can be explained from several theoretical positions. The variety of skilled trades and myriad of markets hardly exempt the industry from the forces of supply and demand or the struggles between economic actors. Yet there are nuances that need to be accounted for, both in their historical development and in their modern forms, which separate the construction industry from the rest of industrialized America.

Modern-day journeypersons could readily trace their craft roots back from present-day mechanics to independent craftspersons to guild members and finally to free artisans. However, the late-twentieth-century waged construction worker is a creation of the capital–labor relationship found in the present age. The hallmark of this period is the wage bargain, which is shaped by a variety of forces peculiar to the market-based construction industry. The skilled and semiskilled journeypersons of the building trades can at times be likened to so many different industrial trades laboring for the completion of one finished product. The product is a completed structure and the production process is carried out at a specific location.

Consider for a moment the analogous development of the needle and weaving trades, in which masters eventually brought skilled journeypersons under one roof and provided them with the means of producing a final product. Construction workers basically possess only the core hand tools of their trades and the skills to use them. Power tools, machinery, and the material are the province of the employee. Yet unlike their weaving predecessors, many tradespeople have no history of craft independence. Although pre–Civil War carpenters and bricklayers could point to such roots, the constructing system arose alongside of technological and market development. In general, the employer contracts with the worker over the specifics of the hours, wages, and conditions of employment, thus giving rise to the notion of the employer as contractor. In essence, the contractor then resells these skills and abilities to the buyer in the form of a finished building product.

So the question should now arise as to how these hours, wages, and conditions are determined. Mainstream economic theory argues that a worker's wage is equal to labor's marginal revenue product (MRP). Given the firm's production function, the market demand, and the market price, it is possible to develop a demand curve for the particular type of labor in question. What separates these wage–employment schedules from each other are the peculiarities of the various markets and trades. The standard labor economic presentations offer a series of demand elasticities that can be expanded or contracted as productivity increases (decreases). It is a basic assumption that firms can identify the output contribution of each labor factor and thus offer wages that reflect the market value of that marginal output. Since firms are profit maximizers, employers are constrained by the market value of their revenue in making their wage employment decisions. The all-important issue for the construction firm and the construction worker is a measurement of the marginal revenue product of an additional labor unit hired. The heterogeneity of skills and outputs found in the industry present the Herculean task of measuring marginal output values.

The process of wage determination has both historic and present-day components. The historic aspect emerges because the modern economic agents have some knowledge of the developed and established market rates. The present-day influence comes out of the relationship to wages of the costs of schooling, training expenditures, subsistence needs, profit margins, and productivity frontiers. The measurement of marginal productivity must be attempted within the complexity of the overall construction industry. Is the iron worker worth more than the plumber? Or the laborer? There are no clearly established parities as may be found in the public sector, but there are clear relationships and bargaining patterns (see McCaffree 1955–56).

Given this background, the ceteris paribus basis for wage expansion relies on fundamental shifts outward in the demand curve for labor. These shifts can come about in two particular ways. One is the case where there is a simple increase in demand for particular tradespersons, such as carpenters or plumbers. In this situation a tight labor market causes wages to rise, similar to the short-run increase in the price of shirts when demand exceeds supply. Open-shop labor markets would adjust wages at each new hire while union shops would alter wages at contract time. The other case is where the demand curve moves in response to productivity increases. Thus if union carpenters could demonstrate in a clear and quantifiable way that they were producing more dollar output per hour than during their previous contract period, there would be a strong basis to demand a wage increase.

The sources of construction productivity have been discussed in earlier chapters. However, it can be seen with respect to wages that there is a basis to mutual advantage from improved levels of output. Higher output is capable of producing a higher marginal revenue product and therefore a higher wage. Increased output is also capable of enhancing the firm's position in terms of revenue and profit.

The wage bargain itself, then, has two settings. It may be concluded through a formal process, as is found in the unionized sector, or it may be made through an informal arrangement, as established by individual worker agreements. Collective bargaining results may recognize the peculiarities of a special trade and they may also be related to the cooperative nature of the industry. In either situation, the wage is a function of the average output per hour. For example, increased output due to technological developments in the manufacturing and pouring of concrete can reward the concrete workers with higher wages. By the same token, these advancements can result in fewer lost hours for other special trades employees, thus improving their productivity.

By and large, union construction agreements ban piecework rates and forms of lumping (lump-sum payments). For example, carpenters' union rules prohibit payment by the board for sheetrock installations, although employers sometimes attempt a bonus pay system based on the number of boards installed per day. While most nonunion carpenters are hired for an hourly rate, they are clearly freer to make piecework arrangements with their employers than union workers are. Piecework itself is related to the physical nature of the trades. Where output is readily quantifiable, there exists a greater possibility of piecework or lumping than in irregular installations (e.g., jobbing work). Thus, a repetitive installation of sheetrock boards allows both parties to calculate piecework or lump-sum payments. A cathedral-style ceiling with a variety of angles would make such counting of the sheetrock pieces far less practical.

In the case of the single worker agreement, wages may be agreed upon informally, for example, by a telephone response to a want ad, or the acceptance of a large firm's list of pay rates. In this situation, the worker's case for above-average pay will be based on a mutual agreement with the employer under the category of merit pay.

Given this overview of the wage-setting process, the specific mechanisms can be explained from a number of different theoretical perspectives. The Smithian notion of market-based wage and price determination most closely reflects the traditional modern nonunion construction labor market. It is marked by easy access to and from the market, individual worker signaling costs, separate firm search costs, good information on area pay rates, and the absence of labor combinations. In the unorganized sector, wages move as labor markets become tight or loose. Supply limitations reflect available skills in the local markets, the willingness of travelers to enter the market, and the specific influences of the local market (e.g., unemployment rates, cost of housing, etc.).

Smithian arguments explaining union wages follow a similar direction. In the union case, an inelastic supply curve limits the existing labor pool under a fixed union wage. A tight labor market would then require union employers to offer overscale payments, leisure incentives, or overtime to induce the extra labor effort needed to complete a project. The union market could also be expanded slightly (short-term) by admitting traveling union workers, union-sanctioned new hires, or newly organized shops.

Theoretically, the Smithian and modern neoclassical explanations apply a basic intuitive logic to wage determination. Yet a number of studies, particularly those explaining union wage movements, have not fully accounted for all of the influences on the wage process.

The institutionalist perspective, with its mainstream basis, and the radical economic view, with its reliance on nontraditional variables, have made important contributions to a further understanding of wage determination. To integrate some of these variables with traditional theories, we must be willing to experiment with the multifaceted social relations of the industry.

Wage determination in the construction industry must be able to incorporate institutional influences such as the Davis–Bacon legislation, trade union threats, and the developing role of the megaconstruction firm. Institutionalists argue that such factors have reshaped the wage bargain to the point where the notions of free market outcomes are no longer realistic.

Classically, the prevailing wage legislation represents the culmination of institutional involvement in the determination of wages. Federal, state, and local legislators are often supported by organized labor, unionized employers, and their political allies. Such laws establish wage-and-benefit percentage minimums that are challenged by non-union employers and free-marketers as abrogating the market system for wage determination.

There is evidence that the longevity of these laws may have a much smaller impact on construction costs than is often cited. Jeff Vincent (1990) has argued that at least in the case of the Indiana prevailing rate laws, the number of unionized construction firms bidding public works would maintain a similar cost factor even without such legislation. At the national level, a study at the University of Utah (Philips et al. 1995) argues that any cost savings are offset by lower income and sales tax revenues (see chapter 7 of this text).

While the prevailing wage debate is discussed in terms of cost inflation, the economic basis of wage floors has a strong Keynesian influence. The visible hand of government has been used to move markets out of stagnant depressed equilibriums since the Great Depression. Inasmuch as prevailing rates are based on weighted local area averages, the pay scales are heavily influenced by local collective bargaining agreements. From a Keynesian perspective, this can be viewed as maintaining worker consumption levels by reducing downward competitive pressures on income.

Although market and institutional analysis have many similarities, radical economists have looked to the social nature of the wage bargain for their insights. With respect to the construction industry, it becomes critical for such economists to establish organic links between the workplace relations and the market price for a skilled tradesperson's knowledge and ability.

David Gordon (1980) has described the limits of unionized workers' collective power. The construction industry has unique structures that tend to augment as well as inhibit the social bonds among workers. The homogenization of skills as represented by specific trades can be a powerful source of union organizing. Day-to-day experiences, work partners, and the cooperative nature of the overall project tend to create worker cohesion.

Collective strength can be a key element to any wage agreement since the wage bargain (collective or individual) is often testimony to negotiating skills as well as productivity measurements. Construction offers a dynamic from within the workplace that can coalesce worker relations around diverse combinations of employees. Connections can be as thin as those established between tool buddies or as thick as those created among all the workers of a trade. In either case, they can serve to enhance wage premiums under specialized job-site conditions such as remote locations, hazardous tasks, and so forth.

The connections that develop through skill and the workplace environment are often weakened by the physical location and layout of the job sites. Points of production are usually atomistic, often scattered from one end of a city to another. The logistics of building construction can frustrate the small employer's control as he or she drives from site to site trying to monitor progress or provide on-site direction. In some cases this can lead to greater workplace control by the firm's employees. These same distances between sites can also separate workers, making union organizing difficult while cutting lines of communication between workers.

Just as the navy is said to euphemistically run on scuttlebutt, so does the construction industry react to informal sources of information. There is a well-established nucleus of reliable information through which decisions concerning development, investment, and employment occur. However, the rumor mills of the trades can readily crank out reports of jobs started, contract negotiation progress, overtime rewards, and impending layoffs that serve as ersatz *Dodge Reports* and BLS fact sheets.

The casual remark at the tavern or on the train ride home can be transformed into hardened fact by the next day's coffee break. In the nonunion market the premium attached to accurate information is far greater than in the union sector. Within the union environment, union meetings, hiring hall lists, and union publications operate as dependable sources of employment information.

Information is an obvious, tangible reward to be gained from being organized. Unions have traditionally cut through the separation of location to unite workers under individual trade banners. Wage determination is a process by which both sides attempt to assess the market value of the skills within the context of the wider economy. Both individual and collective wage bargains depend on accurate information as to the state of the market, relative wages, and external factors such as the cost of living in a particular locale.

It is worth noting that the value of a unified position can be measured not merely by the extensive number of union worker organizations but by the numerous employer groups that have developed over the years. Such trade associations are not limited to union employers but extend to the nonunion sector. In 1994 the Associated Builders and Contractors were able to boast of 174 charter association members from a variety of general and special trades employers (advertisement, *Engineering News-Record,* January 1994).

What is probably most useful in explaining construction wage determination is a clear specification of the variables that influence the hourly wage. Over the years a number of studies have looked at wage determination in both the union and nonunion sectors. From Stephen Sobtoka's study of the Chicago building trades (1953) to H. Gregg Lewis's classic analysis (1963, 1986), there has been a growing dependence on econometric analysis.

Empirical results, as support for underlying theoretical concepts, have suffered from problems with construction statistics. The percentage-organized ratios, unemployment rates, and productivity measures have often proved less than satisfactory for researchers. By briefly drawing again on our three economic theoretical camps, it is possible to develop a more encompassing set of independent variables for wage determination.

In terms of a fundamental understanding of wage changes, it is important to consider real pay-rate movements. Real wages provide a frame of reference as well as an indicator of changes in the employee's standard of living. While trade unionists and employers are often eager to discuss money wage amounts, an analysis of construction wage packages needs to account for inflationary effects.

It is reasonable to expect real wages to be influenced by traditional notions of supply and demand. Both construction unemployment rates and general area unemployment rates can indicate supply levels of workers for available job slots. The effects of unemployment can be blunted by skill levels and unionization, although this will vary across markets. Yet large numbers of reserve workers produce generalized downward pressures across all labor markets while tightness in the excess supply has the opposite effect.

On the opposite end of this pole is the demand for construction. This

Table 11.1

Years of Apprenticeship for Selected Building Trades (New York, NY)

Trade	Years
1. Carpenter	4
2. Electrician	5
3. Elevator constructor	3
4. Ironworker (structural)	3
5. Plumber	5
6. Sheet metal worker	4
7. Steamfitter	5

Source: Apprentice departments of various trades in New York, NY, 1995.

variable can be proxied by the percentage changes in construction employment at either the local or national levels. The Bureau of Labor Statistics and the Census Bureau of the U.S. Department of Commerce have a variety of source materials for this data. Together the supply-and-demand components of an equation help to specify the extent of labor market tightness and its consequent wage pressures.

There has always been a series of arguments that have focused on the skill levels and training costs of learning a trade. Skilled journeypersons, whether they be modern ironworkers or nineteenth-century bricklayers, have often seen their wage demands as commensurate with their specialized abilities. In the family of building trade pay rates, there is to some extent a hierarchy of hourly pay scales that reflects the training, apprenticeships, and general educational levels of workers.

Training and apprenticeship, while closely related to the degree of skill, can serve as a reasonable proxy for skill levels in analyzing the sources of wage change. The list shown in Table 11.1 indicates the years required of a formal union apprenticeship before a worker would attain the highest journeyperson pay scale.

The training periods include work time and vocational instruction under a formal program. As part of the determination of craft wages, the analytical argument is similar to that of the human capital economic position. Training and schooling are seen as, on average, providing lifetime earnings that exceed those returns to similar employees who do not receive such training (see Becker 1983).

Another variable that should be considered in its effect on wages is the safety factor. As an industry topic, safety has always proved particularly nettlesome, and there is much speculation about the net effects of safety in the workplace. From one point of view, lost time and compensable injury rates correlate negatively with wage change. Serious injuries can result in work stoppages and interrupt the flow of the workplace. They involve a cost factor, draining funds that might otherwise go toward the worker's wage package, and the loss of the injured individual's productive services for the duration of the recuperation period. The bottom-line overall effect of lost productivity and the rising costs associated with health care appear as a drain on both the employer's resources and the employee's earnings. The logical conclusion is that safer workplaces foster a more productive environment than job sites that ignore such concerns.

There is some basis for believing that the danger and risk inherent in certain trades is responsible for a wage premium. The National Institute of Occupational Safety and Health (NIOSH) continues to rank the construction industry as one of the most dangerous industries in the country. As in other market systems, one would expect additional compensation to serve as a reward to the rational worker employed in an above-average hazardous job position.

In the eighteenth century, Adam Smith noted the "ardour of the occupation" as one of the determinants of the laborer's wages. Specialty trades often have their own unique dangers built into the work. The sandhog is faced with cave-ins, the ironworker with falls, and the electrician with electrocution. Added to this are general hazards, such as the open shaft or falling debris. It may in fact be the case that intraoccupational wage differentials are due to particular dangers within a certain trade, although it is difficult to define this structure without further empirical research.

In terms of wage dispersion, there is some data available on the extent of pattern bargaining where specific trades act as wage leaders. Some researchers have argued that just as there exist parity arrangements in large municipal union wage contracts, there are wage leaders and followers in the construction industry. Kenneth McCaffree (1955–56) and Martin Personick (1974) found that union wage dispersion was related to movement in key trade negotiations. What may be of equal importance are benefit patterns. As nonenvelope issues increase in significance, some unions tend to play catch-up in bargaining for pensions, health care, and other fringe benefits.

Since collective bargaining agreements are generally signed at the local level, a model explaining wage leadership would need to account for local area conditions. Levels of competition, the efficacy of a union organizing campaign, and the percentage organized would be important variables. This would also add to the complexity of the wage determination model in terms of data collection.

While these various factors represent a considerable number of mainstream arguments for wage determination, the most important influences may well be related to productivity. Theoretically, the singular importance of output per employee hour is a thread that runs throughout all three economic perspectives. The underlying arguments of marginal productivity theory in mainstream theory are mechanically linked to measures of employee output. Keynesian claims for market intervention in order to jump-start economic activity rely ultimately on target levels of output that will attract profit-oriented investment. Finally, nontraditional and radical economists cite productivity issues as a source of friction in the wage bargain.

In an unpublished dissertation by the author (Finkel 1990), productivity was found to have a highly significant influence on the wages of unionized construction electricians in the New York City market. Specifications in that study employed independent variables that served as proxies for national rates of change in construction output per hour. These were based on value put in place per construction worker hour and gross product originating per construction worker hour. The variables were found to have a strong positive influence on electrical worker wage change irrespective of the form of the econometric specification.

There is, however, some dissatisfaction with traditional models of wage determination. Employers and employees are well aware of the human role and social aspects of the wage bargain. The economic climate, when measured by the sum of market factors and job characteristics, can ignore the history of a union's bargaining relation or the specifics of an unaffiliated (nonunion) employer's wage scales. At the minimum, there needs to be an indicator of the employee's role in the bargaining process.

The most widely used measure of worker strength is the percentage-organized statistic. The union proxy variable is used in several forms. These range from the percentage of the labor market that is unionized at a particular moment in time to the number of persons covered by union agreements. As a determinant of the wage, the percentage organized has been shown over a number of studies to be positively correlated with union wage movements. Early studies such as Sobotka's (1953) Chicago Building Trades wage analysis, and more comprehensive works such as those by Lewis (1963, 1986) or Barry Hirsch and John Addison (1986), have employed variants of the percentage union variable. Some researchers have used rates of change to explain wage movements and union/nonunion wage differentials.

Such measures of union strength have been used from different theoretical perspectives. They have been used to hold unions as examples of monopoly market power capable of restricting employment and hiking up wages. Alternatively, these percentages have been seen as benchmarks of union institutional ability to obtain wage–benefit improvements for union members.

These proxy variables for the percentage organized, labor supply, labor demand, and productivity, when linked econometrically, can explain much about wage changes in the construction industry. However, most statistical investigations have been left with substantial residuals of unexplained change in wages. By expanding the model slightly in an effort to capture the social relations in the industry, it is possible to develop a more inclusive specification.

The objective of such an analysis is to avoid a mechanistic approach to wage change where hourly rates react automatically to a specific set of circumstances. While there are reasonably good data for supply, demand, output, schooling, and safety, it is a challenge for the researcher to develop proxies for the social aspects of the wage bargain.

Daniel Mills (1972b) made use of a dummy strike variable while the author (Finkel 1990) extended his mainstream econometric specification to include organizing proxies and a union activism variable. Other researchers such as George Borjas (1979) and Jeffrey Pfeffer and Jerry Ross (1980) have considered wages in terms of job satisfaction and alternative employment possibilities. In his 1980 article on union structure, David Gordon noted the significance of informal work groups and the social bonds created in the workplace.

The upshot is that an analysis of wage determination for the construction industry must consider a wide range of plausible effects. For example, there was a time when the high wages of tradespeople were thought to emanate from the shortened construction season due to weather factors. The argument then inferred that once the physical conditions were created for jobs to operate year-round, the workers maintained their earlier wage premiums.

While there may be some truth to this argument, the real explanations are far more complex. It is incumbent on researchers to weigh the merits of the many variables discussed in this chapter and to consider their impact not merely on money wages but more importantly on the real wage.

CHAPTER 12

Organized Labor and the Building Trades

The role of the unions in the construction industry has a long and interesting history. From its early nineteenth-century roots up to its modern form, the union movement has been a powerful and enduring institution. Its fortunes have waxed and waned with the economics of the industry while union members have helped shape the character of the construction trade itself.

The technical origins of the American building trades unions are found in the cities of the 1790s. Records of the Brotherhood of Carpenters and Joiners indicate early development in Philadelphia, New York, and Boston. John Commons et al. (1936 [1919]) reported the existence of building trades organization memberships as early as 1792, citing their disputes with employers over the pay and conditions of employment.

Like many of the exclusively brethren organizations of the nineteenth century, the construction trade unions were subject to the vagaries of the fledgling market economy. Working within a nation dominated by agriculture, the uneven development of the cities created wide swings in the demand for skilled tradespersons. The limited technological advancement of the pre–Civil War era confined demand to carpenters, bricklayers, stonemasons, and laborers. Such demand was as much affected by North American weather as it might have been by the developing economy. In many ways, the strength of the workers' union reflected the strength of the economy.

The early unions were loose associations of independent craftspersons as opposed to the modern business unions of the twentieth century. They were often formed in response to competition among employers, which tended to drive wages in the direction of competitive pressures. It was an economic climate not unlike the model found in

Adam Smith's *Wealth of Nations*. Small firms, easy market entry, and an exact knowledge of market means, wages, and prices provided a framework for a highly competitive marketplace.

In 1827, Philadelphia painters, glaziers, and bricklayers were reported to have joined carpenters striking for a ten-hour day (Schapner 1975, p. 22). The action gave rise to the local Mechanics Union of Trade Associations, while similar new world organizations began to distinguish between employers (masters) and the journeymen of their trades.

The fits and starts of the trade union movement began to take hold in the skilled trades following the Civil War. In the 1850s, building tradesmen attempted several times to form national organizations, but these ran into numerous difficulties. As with the general labor movement, the tight labor markets of the Civil War provided an impetus to union organizing. There is some indication that the building trade unions helped secure real wage increases during this early period (see Burt 1979; Marshall et al. 1976).

The rise and fall of the National Labor Union (1866–78) and its successor organization, the Knights of Labor, could not sustain consistent support from the ranks of the skilled building trades. Skill homogeneity was a powerful and parochial organizing tool responsible for a narrow view of the nineteenth-century economic and class struggles. The advent of the American Federation of Labor (AFL) in 1886 was a major turning point in the history of the building trades unions.

Many of these trades had organized into local autonomous unions within the larger cities. Loosely, they had developed labor councils that established connections among the various trades. With the focus of the AFL on skilled labor and strong national unions, the building trades unions began to branch out beyond their metropolitan areas. Grace Palladino (1991) provides an example of this in her description of the founding of the International Brotherhood of Electrical Workers (IBEW) in 1891. Emanating from St. Louis, traveling linemen organizers established links with union members across the Midwest. Once a network of electrical unions was created throughout several large cities, the foundation for the forerunner of the IBEW, the National Brotherhood of Electrical Workers (NBEW), was at hand. By 1892 the NBEW was on firm ground as were several other skilled trade national organizations (e.g., painters, carpenters, and bricklayers).

One of the keys to understanding the development of the building trades unions is the membership statistics. The pre–Civil War and

Table 12.1
Construction Union Membership, 1975 and 1995 (thousands)

Union	1975	1995	Percentage Change
Asbestos workers	13	12	−0.08
Boilermakers	123	42	−0.66
Bricklayers	143	84	−0.41
Carpenters	700	378	−0.46
Electrical workers (IBEW)	856	679	−0.21
Elevator constructors	13	20	0.54
Operating engineers	300	298	−0.01
Ironworkers	160	82	−0.49
Laborers	475	352	−0.26
Painters	160	95	−0.41
Plasterers	55	29	−0.47
Plumbers	228	220	−0.04
Roofers*	28	21	−0.25
Sheet metal workers	120	106	−0.12
Totals	3,374	2,418	−0.28

Source: C.D Gifford, ed., *Directory of U.S. Labor Organizations,* Appendix A, 1996, p. 83.
    *1979 membership.

preindustrialization organizations came and went as the economy moved through its cycles. However, the industrialization of the American economy and its subsequent booms brought a new continuity to the building trades movement. As construction became an increasingly important industry in the major cities, so the presence of a local trade-specific union mirrored this permanence.

The periods from World War I through the Korean conflict marked nearly a half-century of solid union growth. Prior to the Wagner Act, building trades union had coalesced around their skill homogeneity. Organizing was a catch-as-catch-can process in which local unions drew their strengths among ethnicities and neighborhood memberships. The formalization of union representation in 1935 established defined bargaining units and means by which building trades unions could organize new shops. The endurance that came from the strength of the building trades in the first thirty years of the twentieth century was finally institutionalized by the Labor Relations Act of 1935.

The maturation of the building trades unions can be seen in Table 12.1. The list of major trade internationals and nationals indicates the peaks and valleys these unions have had during the post–World War II era. Most have experienced declines in membership, which can reflect declines in the demand for services (e.g., plasterers) or technologically induced growth (electrical products manufactured and installed by members of the IBEW). It can also indicate periods of more or less union political power as well as a social climate that influences union membership roles.

The 1992 Bureau of Labor Statistics (BLS) survey of union membership reported 906,000 construction union members. This represented 20 percent of the 4,530,000 workers employed in the industry that year. The percentage was down from 21.1 percent in the previous year and continued a trend that had started in the 1980s. The 1995 BLS survey showed further evidence of the decline, with union membership in the construction industry at 17.7 percent of waged and salaried construction workers.

A declining percentage-organized statistic has several possible explanations. Steven Allen (1985), among others, has argued that the shift in product mix from commercial to residential results in reduced percentages of organized workers. This is because the residential one-family market is typically a highly competitive end of the industry where union skill advantages would not necessarily improve productivity or profitability.

Another factor along these lines has been the shifts in geographic centers of construction activity from strong union areas to weaker ones. For example, if economic activity was to move from the Northeast to the South and Southwest, there would be a commensurate fall in the percentage organized of construction personnel. Many of the southern and western states are right-to-work states and their laws have historically limited union strength and organizing ability.

The role of the building trade unions is possibly best understood through the numerous legal issues pertaining to the construction industry. Although construction unions certainly were beneficiaries of classic pieces of twentieth-century legislation like the Norris–LaGuardia and Wagner acts, a series of industry-specific legal challenges have arisen over the last fifty years.

Probably the most often debated pieces of legislation are the prevailing rate laws. These pertain to a set of wage minimums for public works projects at the federal and local levels. At the center of this issue is the Davis–Bacon Act of 1931, which has served as the model for numerous states' prevailing wage laws (see chapter 7 of this text for a more detailed account).

Critics of these laws generally claim that the creation of an artificial (union-based) wage floor reduces competition and tends to inflate building costs. The assault on public works wage protections has varied from efforts to repeal, to legislation that dilutes the effectiveness of prevailing rate calculations in setting a wage floor. For example, in 1983 the threshold amounts that would kick in Davis–Bacon calculations was raised, while in 1985 legislation was passed that lessened the weighting factor for union wages in figuring the federal prevailing rates.

In rebuttal, unions and their supporters have argued that prevailing wage rates have historically served the public interest. Their claim is that such wage minimums reduce labor strife and provide level playing fields for contractor bids. In addition, they argue that these laws are designed to ensure minimum standards of quality by preventing unscrupulous employers from undercutting the competition with inferior workers.

The debate over the merits of prevailing rate laws has extended to training programs, job descriptions, and helper apprentice ratios. Typically, unions will establish ratios of apprentices to skilled journeypersons. Open-shop and nonunion employers argued for increased use of the helper and trainee classifications at higher ratios than were established in union agreements.

Two particular court cases serve as examples of the political and legal aspects of the helper/apprentice controversy. The first is *Associated Builders and Contractors v. Reich* (1996), a lawsuit filed by the Associated Builders and Contractors (ABC) charging that the Department of Labor (DOL) had failed to put into effect regulations establishing a helper category on prevailing rate projects. Helpers differ from apprentices in their training, schooling, job descriptions, and wage rates. ABC claimed that the lower pay for helpers as opposed to apprentices would yield considerable cost savings for the public sector.

Apprentices are trade specific, and formalized apprentice programs have a variety of costs attached to them. In contrast, helpers may work between trades and can be employed for less-skilled parts of a project. In 1982, the DOL issued helper rules for federal construction projects, which authorized the department to conduct surveys to determine the extent of helper usage in a geographic area. If the use of helpers was found to be a prevailing practice, then the federal construction contracts in that locale would permit the use of lower-waged helpers. As noted in chapter 4, the proposed rule changes developed into an issue of nonenforcement, but the helper dispute is one of primary importance to many skilled building trades unions.

A second court case is also open-ended in its settlement. *California Division of Labor v. Dillingham Construction* (1996) challenged a state prevailing rate law requiring that apprentices be part of a state-certified program. A subcontractor for Dillingham had listed as apprentices employees who were not part of a registered program. The California Department of Labor (CDOL) found Dillingham in violation of the state prevailing rate statute. Dillingham Construction prevailed on appeal to the Ninth Circuit Court, arguing that the findings of the state Department of Labor violated the federal Employee Retirement Insurance and Security Act (ERISA) laws. While the issue is bound for a U.S. Supreme Court hearing, *Dillingham* offers a different argument than simple cost reduction for the public. The use of related pieces of legislation (including those that offer worker protections such as ERISA) to narrowly limit an area of prevailing wage rulings is a trend that will continue develop.

For the most part, the federal prevailing rate legislation has withstood a wide range of challenges. It was suspended in 1971 by President Nixon, who reinstated it following the establishment of the Construction Industry Stabilization Committee. In 1993 Congress raised the threshold at which projects would be subject to the Davis–Bacon requirements to $100,000 for new construction and to $25,000 for repair. Clearly part of the success of prevailing rate is owed to trade union political strength in the face of conservative efforts to repeal.

Equally as important, and technically far more encompassing are the applicable parts of the National Labor Relations Act. One of the most noteworthy construction issues grows out of the 1947 amendment of the National Labor Relations Act known as the Taft–Hartley Act. Section 14(b) of the Act specifically prohibits the requirement of union membership "as a condition of employment in any State or Territory in which such execution or application is prohibited by State or Territorial law." Taft–Hartley did not explicitly ban closed shops but referred this decision to the state legislatures.

Known as the right-to-work provision, the statute has been used successfully to ban the closed shop on construction projects. In a state that has not passed a right-to-work law, collective bargaining agreements can require that all of a firm's employees become union members after a certain date. In the so-called right-to-work states, an employee can receive all the wages and benefits negotiated by the union but need not become a union member. Such legislation is cited as a seriously limiting condition to union power in states that prohibit closed shops. While the building trade unions have from time to time mounted strong repeal campaigns against this law, it, too, like the Davis–Bacon legislation, has survived numerous political and legislative challenges.

There is also considerable attention given to prehire agreements and what are known as project agreements. Prehire agreements are collective bargaining agreements between construction unions and employers made even though the union does not represent a majority of the employer's employees. Provided for under Section 8(f) of the National Labor Relations Act, they essentially represent an exception to the majority status rule because of the unique nature of the construction industry's short-term jobs and skill requirements (Feldacker 1990, pp. 142–43). Under majority status, a union and an employer may enter into agreement only after certifying that the union represents more than 50 percent of the company's employees.

Hypothetically, the XYZ manufacturing company could not sign an agreement with a union until the manufacturer and the union could certify that this was in accordance with the wishes of the majority of XYZ's workers. In the construction industry, a contracting firm could sign an agreement with a union that represented other workers in the same trade without first demonstrating that a majority of the company's workers favored the union.

Project agreements are a form of collective agreement that undergoes considerable scrutiny. The most controversial of these are public works project agreements. In 1993, the Supreme Court upheld the right of the government agency handling the clean-up of Boston Harbor to establish a project agreement for a ten-year construction program. Thus, the Court ruled that when the state acted as the owner, it had the right to make such prehire and collective bargaining agreements part of the bidding process.

The state's interest as the owner is to complete a needed improvement in a timely and cost-efficient manner. Unions offer standardization of holidays, changes in work rules, and no-strike pledges. In a wide range of undertakings, state and local authorities and labor organizations have traded off stability for security to reach a mutually beneficial outcome. The union gets the security of a promise to use union labor while the state receives a guarantee of uninterrupted production.

The objection to these agreements is based on their collaborative nature. They may require an owner to use contractors affiliated with a local building trades organization or employer group. Since these are frequently explicitly or implicitly union associations, unaffiliated contractors claim that an unfair bidding restriction is being imposed.

Alternatively, they argue that such agreements are expressions of union monopoly power that prevent the state from achieving the best (lowest) possible price. The case-by-case application has allowed government bodies to weigh the merits of this bidding procedure. The weakness in this aspect of the open-shop challenge is that an owner is not merely searching for the lowest possible cost but is also considering timeliness, quality, past performance, and labor supply availability.

The 1996 private sector project agreement between Toyota and the Lower Ohio Valley Building Trades Council followed the pattern of this type of agreement for automotive manufacturing plants (Bureau of National Affairs, April 17, 1996, p. 173). Wages were based on those in local area union agreements and the unions agreed to an overall framework of benefits and conditions. The success of the union segment was in part explained by the satisfactory completion of facilities for Toyota in 1986 and for General Motors at its Saturn automobile plant in 1989.

One of the more unique issues facing construction unions and their employers is the question of "double-breasting," or the split shop. In these cases, the same owner operates in both the union market and the nonunion market, depending on the job requirements and level of competition. A contracting outfit may own and operate two distinct shops—one unionized and one nonunion—in the same line of work. This issue is particularly nettlesome to unions since the employer can often steer clear of union agreements by adhering to tests of common ownership, control, management, and separation of facilities. Thus the union and nonunion shop could operate out of the same building with the same principal owners, providing that there were distinct offices, supervisors, employees, and equipment for each of the businesses. Of course, where the construction firm has crossed the line by sharing offices, equipment, and labor between union and nonunion segments, it then becomes known as an "alter ego" and may be forced to operate both firms under the existing union agreement. The practice of double-breasting was facilitated by the 1977 National Labor Relations Board (NLRB) decision in *Peter Kiewit and Sons*, which permitted Kiewit, a very large general contractor, to form a nonunion operation alongside of its union segment.

Some unions have gone to the extent of including prohibitions against double-breasting in their collective bargaining agreements and these have survived court challenges. Double-breasting is not illegal unless a company agrees to withhold from the practice or it develops its nonunion company to the detriment of its existing union employees. In *Painters District Council 51 (Manganaro Corp.)* (1996), the NLRB ruled that anti-dual shop clauses in a union agreement were legally binding. Thus, Manganaro Corp., as a signatory to a painter's union bargaining agreement that contained such a clause, was prohibited from operating as a double-breasted employer. Along the same lines, in *Geiger Ready-Mix Company of Kansas City* (1996), the NLRB ruled that the company had an obligation to negotiate with the union over its reassignment of union work to nonunion workers (Bureau of National Affairs, July 26, 1996, pp. 582–83).

While issues such as pre-hire agreements and prevailing rate laws are of considerable importance to the industry, there are several specific matters that have significant impact on union organizing drives and market power. For example, the simple act of walking a picket line with a placard has been the subject of a number of labor law rulings. Since union picketing has been legally deemed to be more than a First Amendment right of free speech, the purpose, intent, and place of protest must be considered. In the construction industry, a number of fundamental issues related to picketing have been created because of the division and fragmentation of the workplace.

Common situs picketing, that is, the picketing of a common workplace where a number of trades are employed by different employers, is prohibited under the National Labor Relations Act. While picketing the employer's primary place of business is permissible, construction union strike picketing cannot be used to enlist secondary support of fellow tradespersons employed by other subcontractors. Unions have been allowed to picket secondary locations (job sites) under specific limiting conditions, but employers have resorted to gate systems which in essence confine such pickets to nondisruptive locations.

One of the more misunderstood forms of picketing is substandard wage informational picketing. Regardless of union affiliation, an employer paying wages below that of the union's collective bargaining agreement may be the object of lawful picketing. Unions must establish as their primary objective the mere informing of the general public about the level of wages and benefits rather than an attempt to organize the shop in question.

The underlying issues in this type of picketing are related to secondary boycotts and common situs. In their quest to create a union-oriented environment, building trades unions have a long tradition of support for materials and equipment manufactured by unionized firms. At times, the building trades unions have sought to limit the use of equipment produced outside their respective union label areas or outside the generalized union sector of manufacturers. At other times, they have attempted to force subcontractors and employers to purchase goods from union manufacturers. There have also been serious efforts to reduce the use of foreign-produced goods on domestic construction sites. While each of these causes may have its own local champions, union membership popularity, and patriotic appeal, they have all generally run afoul of the secondary boycott prohibitions. The Taft–Hartley secondary boycott rules, the Sherman Anti-Trust Act, the Clayton Act limitations, and the Norris–LaGuardia Act have outlined the framework for judicial review of these activities.

One of the classic precedent-setting cases in the area of union efforts to promote the sale of union-manufactured goods involved construction electricians, their contractors, and the manufacturers of electrical equipment. Known as the *Allen-Bradley* decision, the Supreme Court of the United States argued that Local 3 of the International Brotherhood of Electrical Workers and its unionized employers had attempted to restrain the right to commerce of nonunion and nonlocal electrical manufacturers.

Specifically, Local 3 had "participated with a combination of businessmen," thereby acting in violation of the union exemptions covered by the Clayton and Norris–LaGuardia acts (Feldacker 1980, p. 204). The complexity of the judicial process was narrowed in the end by a 5–4 split decision that focused on marketplace competition. The majority opted to provide relief for the manufacturers by requiring open markets for the sale and installation of their wares irrespective of the union issue.

A further understanding of the construction trade union movement needs to focus on the union as an institutional voice. The underlying hypothesis to the Richard Freeman and James Medoff (1984) compendium is that unions provide means to a collective will that would otherwise fail to exist. Labor law in general protects collective actions in contradistinction to individual workplace protestations. The construction union ties together a homogeneous pool of skilled workers who may be physically dispersed over a large geographic location. Although they may be working for numerous employers, their needs are expressed in a unified position.

From this perspective, it is not difficult to establish a fusible link between the early-nineteenth-century carpenter, the seven-day-a-week rain-or-shine lineman, and the immigrant bricklayer. Construction produces a variety of skills and skill levels. It is also conducted in as diverse a set of physical situations and locations as the sub-zero temperature of the Alaskan tundra and the dry desert heat of the American Southwest. We need only add to this scenario a highly competitive industry, direct employer controls, and a wide latitude in individual management styles. The resulting mixture is one that has historically led workers to seek defined job responsibilities, reduced inter-worker competition, and wages commensurate with their skill levels and training.

David Gordon (1980) has noted that union strengths are likely to develop as a function of skill homogeneity. Although construction and alteration jobs can be widely scattered workers are linked by a variety of relationships. The cooperative nature of the construction project and the importance of skill in determining levels of output have been instrumental in creating tight-knit and powerful local unions.

While the preceding discussions have pointed to a number of sources of declining union membership, the history of the skilled building trades has been vocal, visible, and enduring. Higher-waged specialty trades have been successful in developing strong international unions that are able to solidify and direct union activity. The Committee on Political Education (COPE) works as a lobbying arm for the building trades and receives its funding primarily from union membership contributions. These activities can be combined with pockets of intense local union campaigns to create a network of worker strength capable of offsetting losses in membership numbers.

The concept of the autonomous local union has diversified union influence on the industry. The many facets of involvement, from wages to legislation, have helped to firm up the local union chapters' presence in spite of economic fluctuations. Although collective representation has been by far the most significant union role, the organized-labor component of the training process has in many ways underscored the entire union/nonunion debate. These distinctions will be examined in the next chapter.

CHAPTER 13

Construction Industry Training

The training process in the construction industry has a variety of special characteristics. Depending on the market and the job title, a wide range of formal and informal mechanisms are used as training aids. In the simplest example, the nonunion labor market can depend almost exclusively on job-site training with the employee purchasing a minimum of vocational schooling prior to being hired. On the other end of the training spectrum lies the union sector with its formalized apprentice training programs that generally feature a mix of on-the-job training and off-site vocational classes.

During the post–World War II era the state has become increasingly involved in the guaranteeing and administration of apprentice training. Certification of apprentice training programs has been linked to government contract awards, while the state has claimed a responsibility to ensure fairness in the distribution of apprenticeship positions. As construction technologies change toward the end of the twentieth and the beginning of the twenty-first centuries, formalized training continues as an increasingly important issue for employers and workers alike.

To understand the background of construction training programs, it is helpful to consider vocational training in the light of human capital theory. This is tantamount to hypothesizing that construction workers and their employers are willing to invest certain sums of money (or time) given a set of internal rates of return on these investments. Such returns are related to the various skills and the learning curves for acquiring them. Consequently, general construction skills such as basic laboring may have short-run rates of return that are higher when compared to more technical trades. The payoff to the skilled specialist or heavy equipment operator should be in the form of a higher lifetime earnings benefit as opposed to lifetime income from a less skilled position.

The arguments concerning training typically reflect the notion that training can be either specific or general. The usual position is that generalized training is a cost borne by the employee while firm-specific training may be paid for by the employer. In basic economic terms, the returns of generalized training are more readily captured by the employee while firm-specific educational returns are more easily retained by the company. Gary Becker's groundbreaking work (1975) provides the classic economic overview of the investment in on-the-job training. Becker's work takes into account the issues of marginal training costs in relation to marginal wage increases. The basic economic assumptions of the wage equaling the marginal revenue product $(w = MRP)$ are fully adhered to by arguing that the wage plus the associated marginal training costs are equal to the marginal revenue product plus the present value of the time spent in training. In short, the value of the trained worker's output will cover the wage plus the stream of training costs.

With its extensive system of indentured apprenticeships and state-monitored training programs, construction training provides a mixture of specific and generalized skill improvements. However, within the construction industry there are a variety of schemes by which training costs are shared by both employers and employees.

Becker (1983, p. 35) cites examples of carpentry training, noting that while such costs are usually paid by the trainee, firms sometimes cooperate in paying the costs of apprentices. The thing to note in the construction industry is that there are both formal and informal apprenticeships, trainee programs, and distinctions between the union and nonunion markets.

Modern apprenticeships are technically indentured contracts, which in most areas require state certification or approval. The apprenticeship arrangement has its historical roots in the master–artisan–journeyman relationship. In colonial America the agreement took on the properties of near slavery conditions in which the indenture agreement required an absolute servile existence under a given master. One could logically argue that the limited productivity of the indentured apprentice was offset by the subsistence duties of cleaning, cooking, and agricultural chores. Similarly, there were long periods of such training (e.g., fourteen years) that would provide a time horizon during which marginal outputs could rise to the point where masters could capture a return on their investment. The value of the marginal product created through training could be equilibrated with future marginal revenues as apprentices learned their trades.

Apprenticeships of the late twentieth century generally run from four to five years, depending on the specifics of the trade and market conditions. There are annual promotions with attendant pay raises as the apprentice moves toward journeyperson status. The apprentice forgoes the present higher income that could be earned from alternative employment in return for the eventual higher pay of a building tradesperson.

A more salient consideration from the employer's perspective is the issue of capturing future returns. Since by nature construction produces considerably high levels of labor turnover, even firm-specific training rewards can be difficult to maintain. However, a combination of labor market attachment and a sharing of trained employees can sharply reduce lost returns of training costs.

In the unionized sector of the industry, jointly (management and union) run apprentice programs and union-directed programs have limited such training investment losses. By virtue of the organized sector's benefit structure, there is an induced reluctance on the part of union workers to leave the union sector and forgo their health and welfare benefits.

At the same time, union/employer training programs produce workers with similar sets of skills who move only within the unionized sector. Thus, employers who have contributed training moneys on behalf of an employee who is subsequently laid off can readily expect to receive a future employee who is at least as productive as the laid-off worker.

While the nonunion sector can also create formalized and certified programs, their labor market outcomes are less clearly defined. In the case of the individual employer, all nonemployee-borne costs are the sole expenditure of the firm. There is no guarantee of a replacement worker who has undergone similar types of training and can fit into the company's method of installation.

Probably one of the real hidden distinctions between the union and nonunion sectors lies in on-the-job training (OJT). The hands-on nature of construction and the uniqueness of project settings require considerable hours of field training. While formal apprenticeships contain field-hour criteria for advancement, the logic of construction training dictates extensive amounts of OJT in both union and nonunion settings.

The issue that arises is who will provide that instruction. As in any pedagogical situation, the quality of instruction is related to a large degree to the quality of the instructor. It is reasonable to argue that the more competent and qualified the journeyperson, the higher the caliber of the OJT. It would then be expected that employers or industry segments using formally trained workers would, ceterus paribus, have more effective on-site training programs than those firms using informally trained personnel.

Since on-the-job training depends heavily on one worker's imparting knowledge to another, such training programs must contain an efficient means of transferring skills and information. Given the limited number of job openings, there is often a reluctance on the part of skilled journeypersons to train their eventual competition. For this reason, apprenticeship training should be considered in the context of hiring practices and job security.

In the informal, nonunion sector, training often takes place on an ad hoc basis. Employers hire to fill specific job requirements with occasional long-term opportunities. New hires and existing employees are subject to the movements of the market in terms of demand for their services. New employees can be viewed as threats to present employees regardless of latter's longevity. In the situation where instruction is carried out by the journeyperson who is also the employer, such threats are obviously absent. However, there is still a constant concern for recouping any time and money put into training new personnel even in the smallest of shops.

A merit-based or open-shop contractor will often use a variety of training programs to create the necessary skills. Employers such as those who are part of the Associated Building Contractors rely in part on educational programs funded through their association. Skill development can range from trade-specific to generalized helper categories in which the individual assists several different types of construction workers. In such generalized cases, the threat to the skilled craftsperson's employment is reduced because advancement is not automatic for these helpers. However, when merit shop hiring is based on increased demand, existing employees may be hesitant to train their potential replacements. Since open-shop employees have no influence on the hiring process, the pool of job competitors is a function of the employer's market demand.

The formalized apprenticeship programs of the union sector have indirectly addressed the issue of job security through the collective bargaining agreement. Since many building trades unions use apprenticeship as a means of monitoring the available labor supply, unionized workers have representation in determining future levels of competitive employment pressure. While no doubt unionized workers may under certain conditions feel some of the same unwillingness to train new hires as their nonunion counterparts, they at least have a collective voice and a basis for diminishing those concerns.

Another consideration is the fact that most union journeypersons, and particularly specialty trades workers, have gone through an apprenticeship program themselves. Thus, the socialization process presents OJT as a normal part of the workplace routine. This develops an understanding on the part of existing employees of the need for new workers and an overall acceptance of these potential competitors.

At the same time, many unions negotiate limits on the use of apprentices as well as the process for graduating to journeyperson status. In the case of jointly managed training programs, regulation of the labor supply is a typical element of the collective bargaining process. Where the union itself manages the apprenticeship, it may exercise greater control by virtue of its role as gatekeeper to entry-level positions.

A final note about jointly managed training programs is that both employers and union officials monitor training and require progress reports. In some trades, job rotation is instituted for the purpose of gaining additional experiences. It then becomes incumbent on the union journeyperson to view on-the-job training as a standard part of his or her regular employment duties.

The overall importance of such on-site programs and formalized apprenticeships has been recognized since the passage of the Fitzgerald Act in 1937. Put into law as part of the depression-era social-economic legislation, the act required vocational mandates intended to safeguard apprentices and promote standardization for industry training. It helped to establish a nationwide standard for training in apprenticeable jobs including the building trades. The U.S. Congress further supported this formalized industrial training with the enactment of the Vocational Education Act (George–Barden) in 1946. Specifically, this act provided for a first appropriation of $8 million for vocational trade instruction.

While the passage of this legislation came during a period of union strength, it was seen as a way of producing the skilled workers needed for periods of future economic growth. The law was also responsible for providing a structure to many already existing apprentice programs that lacked clear procedures for advancement or curriculum development.

Modern state-certified apprentice requirements now include mandated hours of on-the-job experience and classroom instruction. Thus, annual advancements and pay increases in a typical union apprentice program are predicated on the completion of these requirements.

State apprentice boards monitor union and nonunion apprentice programs and can review, certify, and decertify programs based on the content, structure, and procedures of the various plans. States will often review the apprentice selection process to ensure fairness in the filling of these entry-level positions.

One of the important aspects of the apprentice program is the selection process for new applicants. State apprentice committees often monitor this process. In many instances this monitoring has followed wide public demand that job enrollments be devoid of hereditary hiring lists or family legacies as were used in the bygone era of "father and son" trade unions. The objective is to ensure that these bottom-line jobs are filled in a nondiscriminatory fashion with respect to gender, race, and age. In trades where there have been industry affirmative action plans, apprentice programs are often required to conform in their final selection to reflect the racial composition of the local area work force. The process also requires that certain numbers of entry-level positions are available to female applicants under the same local-area work-force criteria.

Classroom instruction, administration, and recruitment are all industry costs. For this reason, an important economic issue in terms of apprenticeships is the funding of the program itself. While government has shown an interest in promoting vocational training since the Smith–Hughes Act of 1917, apprentice programs are generally privately funded. Typically, a union agreement will include contributions to a training fund that is administered either by the union or by a joint committee of employers and employees. In some cases the state will provide training moneys for some aspects of the program and this varies from state to state.

The hours for classes and field experience vary among the different trades, but successful completion of the work/class assignment is a determining factor in advancement up the job ladder. The progression entitles apprentices to wage increases as they move toward journeyperson status. In the unionized apprentice training programs, the pay increases are subject to the collective bargaining agreement while the general hour requirements are linked to state-established time periods.

While minimal skilled-trade information can be passed on in a vocational high school program, the heart of trade-specific training is found in the combination of on-the-job and classroom instruction. These programs are designed to meet the average skill needs of the respective skilled trades. As such, they can produce adequate numbers of skilled workers to fill future needs in the building trades. There is a considerable savings for employers through a reduction of search costs. By drawing only from the pool of similarly trained workers, employers avoid the skill unknowns that come with the transience of the construction industry.

For the employee there is the benefit of lowered signaling costs when looking for employment. Union apprentice programs often contain referral systems or hiring hall programs that match industry labor supply with its demand. In the cases where workers find their own employment, the apprentice certification informs prospective employers of their skill levels.

Technologically, apprentice programs provide all parties with a formal means to introduce changes in construction installation and practice. By virtue of the course curriculums and job rotation, apprentices are exposed to a variety of construction tools and materials. While construction as an industry may historically have a slow track record in terms of change, its training programs are capable of moving in step with any significant technological shifts.

An ancillary effect of apprentice training is to develop the mechanism for journeyperson retraining. Many unions and some Associated Builders and Contractors (ABC) employers have used their expertise from apprentice and helper programs to create classes for journeymen and journeywomen. Classes have ranged from instruction on fiber-optic installations (electrical and communications workers) to hazardous material handling (laborers) to basic literacy for the purpose of improving reading skills.

The use of formal apprenticeship training also provides employees with a clear sense of their career advancement. By replacing arbitrary

or discretionary promotion with rudimentary job ladders, training programs help to reduce workplace friction and improve worker morale.
While there are no specific studies that have focused on building trades
programs, there are numerous studies that have linked job satisfaction
with formal progression and advancement (see Borjas 1979). The relationship between turnover and worker expectations is an additional
reason why open-shop employers have started to focus on more formalized training (e.g., the ABC-supported National Center for Construction Education and Research).

An equally important training issue is the question of minority labor
force participation. While this was once relegated to the category of
racial discrimination, it has more recently expanded to include the
issue of female employment in the building trades. The discrimination
problem is related specifically to training because it is clear that decent
pay and skilled job opportunities are linked to extensive vocational and
on-the-job training. Therefore, the barriers to entry-level positions can
produce workplace friction and output inefficiencies.

Institutionalized discrimination in the overall economy has been a
serious and pervasive cause of economic disadvantage among minority
households (Marshall et al. 1976, p. 522). A complex web of apprentice job barriers, educational prerequisites, and racial prejudice led to a
difficult and protracted struggle for employment opportunities for minority workers. Since there is a considerable hourly rate differential
between the union and nonunion sectors, the focus of this dispute has
generally been on the union positions.

Following passage of Title III of the 1964 Civil Rights Act, the
federal government moved to expand minority employment on feder-
ally financed projects. Under the concept of affirmative action, federal
construction contracts required job-site employment percentages by
race and more recently by gender.

The question of racial quotas and racial discrimination, when considered in economic terms, can be seen as an outgrowth of the forces
of competition. The nature of this competition is found in the employment markets as well as the product markets. For example, in the union
sector the competition between workers is mediated by the standardization of pay, hours, and conditions as prescribed by the collective
bargaining agreement. Such contracts usually include a hiring procedure that should serve to reduce arbitrary hiring and whimsical firing.
The institutionalization of this process can act as a buffer against dis-

criminatory hiring by the employer. Of course, the more pertinent issue
has been whether or not the institution itself (e.g., the union) has mani-
fested discriminatory membership policies.

In the building trades as in many occupations, the working-class
search for a family legacy has often revolved around the inheritance of
an employment opportunity in the absence of any material riches. The
father-and-son concept of many building trades epitomized this social
phenomenon particularly in the face of the cyclical swings of the construction market. This needed only to be combined with the pressures
of unemployment to produce the most horrific of barriers to labor
market entry—racial prejudice. The low labor participation rates for
minorities could be accounted for by de facto or intentional discrimination. Such virtual controls were removed voluntarily by many unions,
while other unions' restrictive plans fell under court supervision.

The 1962 apprentice class of Local 3 of the International Brotherhood of Electrical Workers has been cited as an example of groundbreaking direction for the building industry. The New York City
construction electricians' union, under the leadership of Harry Van
Arsdale Jr., actively recruited minority applicants into a largely white
male apprentice training program (Mills 1972b, pp. 162–63).

The subsequent improvements in minority employment were miti-
gated by the continual volatility of construction employment. The rise
in the late 1960s and 1970s of self-professed job placement groups for
minority workers led to a near quarter-century of violence and intimi-
dation. The high urban minority unemployment rates and the scarcity
of well-paid blue collar jobs have continually served to fuel friction
between the employed and the unemployed. As part of public efforts to
create minority employment, many states have linked bid awards to the
instituting of entry-level guarantees for high school students. With
many minority students taking vocational classes, programs such as
Project Pathways in New York State required bidders to accept a spec-
ified number of applicants to its training programs from these types of
secondary schools.

The challenge to create employment for minority men has often
been the focal point of these jobs programs. However, there has been a
strong effort by several women's organizations to gain entry into numerous male-dominated hard-hat trades. Although female construction
employment started to rise in the mid-1970s, the recession of the late
1970s served to temper these gains. In addition, the dearth of construc-

tion job opportunities furthered male resistance in both hiring and training, and these attitudes have often proved to be a stronger barrier than the ruggedness of the work.

One recent response to minority construction participation has been the creation of economic development zones. Under this structure, public contracts are allotted to employers with employees from within the development zone. Since these zones are located in depressed communities, the approach is intended to increase economic activity for residents of these local areas. Some cities' economic development zones have attempted to tailor efforts to ensure minority-firm participation in the local construction economies.

The building trades have never been immune to the various socio-economic forces operating throughout society. Steeped in tradition, yet buffeted by emerging social and technological change, the construction industry has formulated a unique set of responses to ever-changing circumstances. The industry's training programs, vocational schooling, and formal apprenticeships need to be considered in that context.

CHAPTER 14

Safety Concerns

Safety has always been an important issue within the building industry. Whether it is a question of cost, a productivity debate, a public concern, or a catalyst to workers' actions, safety is an ever-present consideration. Construction workers are constantly threatened with danger and injury due to their intense physical involvement and the obvious precariousness of any construction project. In an average year, everyday lifting, carrying, rigging, and the multitude of hand and arm movements can be responsible for a wide range of personal injuries. Hands-on operations involve turning, twisting, and cutting with hardened steel tools such as screwdrivers, pliers, and hammers. These are used in addition to a long list of hand-held power tools needed for the numerous small-scale day-to-day activities. From quarter-inch chuck electric drills to gasoline-powered Carborundum blade saws, each tool comes with its own unique safety requirements.

Compounding the inherent dangers of these tools are the arenas in which their use occurs. In new construction work, many employee hours are spent in unprotected areas with considerable exposure to falling objects and debris. Shafts, precipices, and facades are all danger zones. Entire workplaces high above the ground, like a skyscraper's steel grid or a river dam's concrete wall, become isolated sites of latent danger. Added to these settings are the impediments of the natural environment. In urban areas, the endless problems of heat, cold, rain, and wind can produce mayhem on any project manager's schedule sheet. In nonurban settings, mountainous terrains, deep waters, and floodplains can each require specific and costly measures for securing worker safety.

There is also apprehension about construction materials and building systems. While each material and service has a specific function or use, each has attached to it a set of unique cautions. Insulation composed of asbestos and fiberglass or modern mineral fibers is a classic example of an actual and potential workplace hazard. Electricity yearly fells hundreds of workers by electrocution, while many trades face dangers associated with high-pressure steam lines, welding tanks, and mechanical equipment.

Finally, there is the often neglected but important issue of job sanitation. The site itself often takes on the look of the world's messiest room, replete with a staff of willing laborers ready to clean at a moment's notice. Yet the orderly removal of rubbish and debris is a significant facet in the financial and technical success of any project. From washup areas to lavatories to changing and staging areas, the problem of personal hygiene can significantly impact the bottom line of a project.

Although the construction job site is filled with hazardous situations, it is also peopled by skilled employees, who are not oblivious to these problems. Training programs, related employment experience, and apprenticeships are important elements in controlling for site injury rates. The construction learning experience includes a great deal of on-the-job instruction. The notion of "baptism by fire" varies by trade, type of installation, and requisite skill levels. Logically, the operation of specific machine and hand tools necessitates a certain degree of familiarity in order that an assignment be completed in a timely fashion. Job-site injuries are not merely a threat to the worker's earning ability, but can negatively impact a firm's profitability.

For these reasons, overall training periods take on the characteristic of an apprenticeship, whether formal or informal. Instruction can range from lessons on basic hammering to complex drilling using magnetically held drill motors equipped with diamond drill bits. Thus, there is an important time horizon required for producing fully competent journeypersons. While there may be disputes about lengths of specific training requirements, it is apparent that an understanding of construction site routines must be developed through on-site tutorials.

Since skill development and safety problems represent a cost to the employer, the role of technology is twofold. On one side, there is a search for safe equipment that will reduce workers' exposure to workplace hazards. On the other side, there is the fact that the de-skilling process can inherently create safer construction sites through elimination of intricate but dangerous work assignments.

By the late 1960s the rising industrial injury rates became significant enough to warrant the establishment of the Occupational Safety and Health Administration (OSHA) in 1970. This federal agency is charged with the monitoring of a wide range of job-site safety and health standards through on-site inspections and investigations. As the central federal safety agency, OSHA can impose fines and sanctions on violators.

With the creation of OSHA came a revamping of the data-gathering process with respect to job-site safety. While the new statistical measures provided greater accuracy in determining injury and accident rates, changes in the measurement process brought about statistical inconsistencies. An early post–World War II series accounted for a variety of injuries and the percentages of workers effected. Although the studies were not conducted for every year in the 1950s and 1960s, they did provide a coherent set of data for comparative analysis.

In 1971, measurements were changed to reflect the requirements of the Occupational Safety and Health Act. The law as written made an effort to establish baselines for comparison in a variety of occupations and for different types of injuries. In establishing categories for serious injuries, and compensable and lost-time accidents, OSHA was able to provide a realistic and consistent statistical picture of industrial safety.

At the state and local levels, there is an absolute dearth of construction safety data. In some cases, injury rates are reported as part of a survey or as they relate to another statutory program such as workers' compensation or disability. Clearly cost-conscious legislators may be prone to cut funding for surveys and data collection. In addition, esoteric studies promoted by special-interest groups can lead to helter-skelter statistical series. States such as Wyoming, the birthplace of workers' compensation, and more industrialized states such as New York, have solid time series data for recent years, while they often lack consistent historical data. Although many states have conducted a wide variety of studies, even the best industrial series seldom break down their data to the four-digit standard industrial classification (SIC).

The construction site is generally regarded as one of the most dangerous industrial settings. The 1990–91 BLS estimates of occupational injury and illness found that construction had the highest incident rate of all sectors for total cases of lost workdays. Thus, there has developed a fairly contentious debate over the path to reducing construction-related injuries.

In economic terms, the safety issue can bounce back and forth between predictable polar extremes. A safe workplace can be seen alternatively as an untenable cost, a productivity enhancement, an imposition on the free market, and a question of employee rights. The construction industry has managed to develop its own special scenarios for each of the above categories.

Safety can represent a significant cost for any employer. In the form of tools, training, and job-site procedures, the safe workplace is an additional dollar amount added to the cost of a project. In the form of certifications for hazardous-material handlers, the safe workplace can become a generalized cost as well as a portable skill embodied in the individual worker.

One way to examine the cost issue is to consider safety-associated expenditures as capital outlays. That is, the cost of training a worker to handle asbestos or the price of a face shield should be seen in the same manner as the cost of apprentice training or the price of a drill. The basic underlying competitive market assumption is that marginal cost must equal marginal revenue.

Under the classic presentation of the cost–revenue equivalency, construction firms will be willing to provide investments in safety technologies provided there is a return to such investments consistent with the returns on alternative investments. In addition, the rates of return must be similar to the rates expected where no specialized safety costs are incurred. Thus, a renovation project involving asbestos abatement must exhibit the same or greater profitability as a new school project involving typical hazards and dangers for the industry.

Making safety pay for itself is no mean feat. To many building trades employers, the web of certifications, governmental regulation, and enforcement procedures creates an environment hopelessly lost to lower profit margins and bureaucratic interference. Safety-related expenses are seen as an erosion of their competitiveness or a pervasive loss of workplace control.

There are unfortunately a host of economic factors that can delay the implementation of safety measures. In particular, the construction industry is composed of many small and mid-sized companies that find short-term costs for short-term projects to be a severe economic encumbrance. As has been noted by the AFL-CIO's Center to Protect Workers' Rights, the U.S. construction industry lags behind its foreign counterparts in the use of numerous innovations such as the two-handed screwdriver and smaller sized drywall (*Wall Street Journal,* February 22, 1994, A1:5). In order to gain business acceptance there needs to be a leveling of site safety costs for competitive reasons. Legislated job-site safety is viewed by employers as a system that can at times punish the low bidder. For example, a contractor may find after construction is well under way that his site safety supervisor is lacking in proper certifications or years of experience.

Mainstream economic theory argues that there must be an economic incentive for employers to accept new technologies, regulations, or installation methods. Thus, every additional dollar spent on safety must produce at the minimum a dollar in revenue. The expenditure can be viewed in three ways. The first is to consider safety as a final cost that must be passed along to the end user of construction services. In this respect, the end product user shoulders the ultimate cost of safety improvements in her contractual payments. Such price increases are affected by state regulations and the state's diligence in enforcement so as to smooth out the competitive aspects of these increases in the cost of business.

The second way to view the expenditure on safety is that it can result in a return based on lower insurance premiums, rebates, or reduced statutory penalties administered by the state. Increased savings associated with investments in safety can be attributed to lower lost-time accident records. As workers become more secure in their workplace environment, their productive capabilities are enhanced as they work without the interruptions caused by injuries. Fall protections, ground fault shock protectors, and improved job-site hygiene remove impediments to on-site mobility and effort. While there has only been minimal analytical work in this area, there is indication of positive returns for employers and employees (Sider 1983; Arno 1984).

The third interpretation of safety costs can be expressed through the benefits to production of reduced job-site injury rates. Safety as an investment has the potential to offer a payoff for both workers and employers. We need only apply the same standards to safety training and equipment that are applied to skill training and capital outlays. This should involve the notion of research and development as well as time horizons necessary to recoup the original investment.

Training expenditures can also be treated as human capital investments allowing employees to become more productive at certain tasks while reducing injury-related claims and lost workdays. Such training may be job-specific or generalized industry instruction. For the employer, the most onerous of these costs are those that occur on short-term projects staffed by temporary help. The cyclical nature of the industry can prevent reassignment of these new hires, thereby interrupting the repayment period on the investment in specialized safety training and equipment.

Safety can also be facilitated by the basic substitution of capital for labor, which provides machinery to carry out some of the least desirable and more hazardous duties. As in any capital-for-labor trade-off decision, the use of trenching equipment, digging equipment, or chopping machinery must be cost-effective. The capital–labor substitution is linked to profit margins as much as it is to any value judgments about a safe workplace. Of course, the same safety issue leads to a problem of worker acceptance of new technologies.

Not coincidentally, the safety industry has spawned its own specialized areas such as ergonomics, industrial hygienics, and occupational therapy. These have grown in part out of a changing social respect for the environment, organized labor's push for safety legislation, government intervention, and insurance liabilities.

Typical of these specialized areas are compliance requirements developed at the state or local level. In California, the Division of Occupational Safety and Health (DOSH) held a series of hearings in 1993 and 1994 to determine ergonomic standards pertaining to training and labeling information (Bureau of National Affairs, March 9, 1994, pp. 26–27). While that particular set of standards was mandated by a California workers' compensation law, the topic of workers' compensation has been an integral part of the overall safety question.

Workers' compensation began its role in providing statutory payments in 1911. First passed in Wyoming, and subsequently passed by every state legislature, the compensation program is part of the social welfare net established for workers in numerous industries. While payments can vary from state to state (and even industry to industry), the issues surrounding this topic are remarkably similar to safety regulation debates.

Compensation payments are generally funded through employer contributions. Although required by statute, such payments appear to the employer as a cost of doing business. There is an interest in keeping premium payments to a minimum, and this can be reflected in the level of benefit payments. For the employees, such payments are seen as part of their benefit structure and their social safety support. As mediated by state legislatures or employer/employee–managed programs, the payout amounts can reflect intense political or contractual bargaining agreements.

There is ample justification for the argument that improved construction safety programs and regulations can reduce compensation costs. Workers and society are better served when employees receive job-related income rather than injury-related compensation. Yet this, too, opens up an area of great concern. The constant threat and wide variety of construction-site hazards are mixed with an employment picture of severe instability. Thus, states with liberal compensation programs and weakened oversight procedures can invite fraudulent claims as an alternative to construction unemployment. This can be paralleled by the possibility of increases in job-site accidents as construction workers become less risk-averse in an effort to stay employed. In 1994, the Federal Advisory Commission of the National Council on Compensation Insurance estimated that fraudulent claims could account for 25 percent of all compensation reports (Bureau of National Affairs, April 27, 1994, p. 147).

An innovation in compensation plans has been the development of alternative dispute resolution (ADR) programs. The impetus for these plans stems from rising compensation costs, delays in benefit payments, and a long series of expensive courtroom litigations. Under a typical ADR process, an injured employee first contacts an adviser and then a mediator for a determination of compensation. In the event of a dispute, the plan moves quickly into binding arbitration.

Model compensation plans have been developed in a number of states and by a number of unions and employers. The benefit to the worker is that there has been a marked decrease in time between injury and payment. The advantage to the employer is a decrease in overall premium payments and attorneys' fees. In California, the National Electrical Contractors–International Brotherhood of Electrical Workers ADR Trust claimed to reduce premiums by 50 percent. It also reported a strong decline in the number of claims, although quicker settlements may be accompanied by slightly lower benefit payments (Bureau of National Affairs, June 12, 1996, p. 455). ADR has been used for some time in the risk management aspects of the design and engineering segment of the industry. The adaptation of this process to workers' compensation is a novel approach to a long-standing industry concern.

The economic factors of the industry become intertwined with the practice of creating a safe workplace. What is the best means of developing a nonhazardous work environment? Would legislated safety observer meetings and on-site safety engineers prove effective in terms of injury reduction and affordable procedures?

The field of job-site safety is in itself an important political issue. With the creation of OSHA, organized labor and organized business groups tussled over various pieces of safety legislation. Since OSHA can penalize employers and in some cases employees for safety infractions, their job-site presence and procedures can affect a firm's operation and costs directly at the point of production.

Federal review of the safety standards for the construction industry can be found in OSHA publications written specifically for the building industry. The detailed requirements for everything from hard hats to overhead protection for tractor operators have become part of the standard compliance activities for all construction projects. The expansion of regulations to hazardous materials and confined spaces has served to bring a semblance of uniformity in the treatment of many common dangerous building conditions.

The standards established by OSHA for the construction industry are spelled out in Part 1926 of the Code of Federal Regulations (CFR). By definition, *construction work* means "work for construction alteration, and/or repair, including painting and decorating." The Williams–Steiger Occupational Safety and Health Act of 1970, which went into effect in 1971, created a far-reaching safety consensus for a number of different industries.

The same process also occurred at the state and local levels. Environmental protection agencies and a slew of government departments have shown significant interest in managing toxic substances and hazardous situations. For the construction industry, this has led to numerous certifications and testing procedures.

From an industry standpoint, the fundamental issue is whether or not the safety regulations raise costs for construction work. Administratively, regulatory requirements clearly raise the cost of doing business. Office paperwork, on-site reporting, and data collection are time-consuming tasks that must be taken into account.

Added to the cost of safety are accident prevention programs and corrective actions. Everything from electrical grounding to the erection

Figure 14.1. **The Demand for Safety**

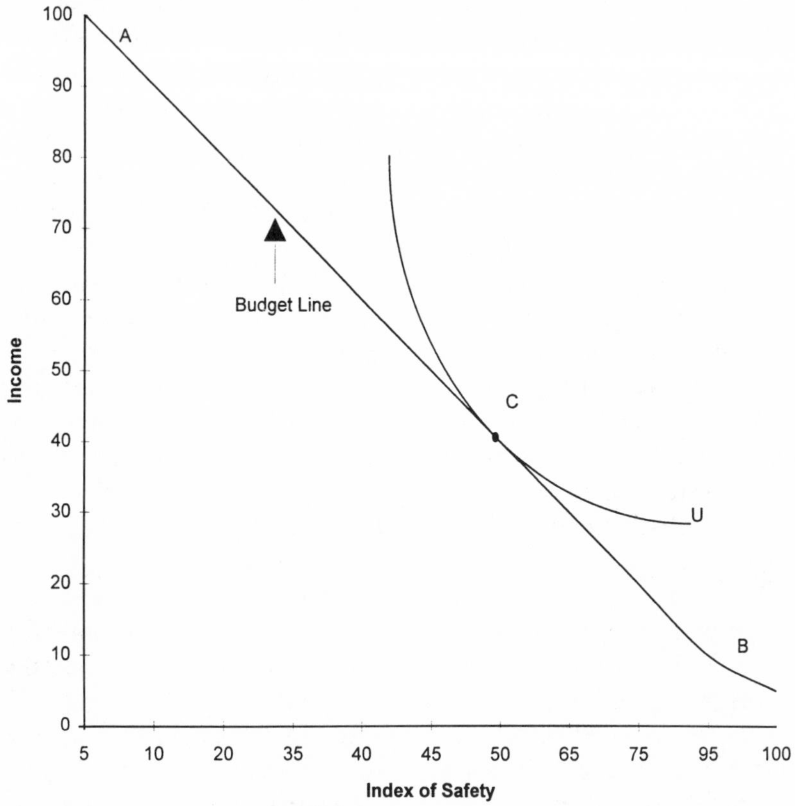

Source: Adapted from Hirshleifer 1976, p. 138.

and maintenance of perimeter barriers requires expenditures of resources and hours. If the installations are found not to be in compliance with safety codes, then on-site inspections can compound the costs through fines and shutdowns

In terms of microeconomic analysis, the costs of safety must be equalized by the revenues accruing to the project as a result of the safety programs. The most simplistic view would be to argue that safe workplaces are more productive workplaces and therefore the marginal cost of safety is balanced by the marginal revenue product of the safer worker. To take matters a step further, the situation could be integrated into the classical diagram of the demand for safety as portrayed in Figure 14.1.

In this perspective, *AB* is the budget line boundary that defines the worker's opportunity set. The worker can "purchase" more safety by giving up income, or gain income by working in less safe employments. *U* is an indifference curve that demonstrates combinations of safety and income preferred by a worker. The optimum, point *C*, is a point on the indifference curve that is just tangent to budget line *AB*. At this point, the preference for safety and income are equal to the combinations of income and safety actually obtainable. There is a tradeoff between the *x* axis of an index of relative safety and the *y* axis of dollar amounts of hypothetical hourly incomes. Given the possible pay rates for a specific job and the worker's personal preferences for safety (income), a point of satisfaction, *C,* is attained.

Two arguments are possible. One is that as job sites become safer, workers' incomes will be reduced as the premium for hazardous employment is reduced. Essentially, the worker purchases safety by sliding downward on budget line *AB*. This raises the question of the real source of funding for on-site occupational health and safety improvements.

An opposing outcome is that marginal productivity in the less dangerous workplace rises to the point at which workers' incomes increase. The higher level of income gained from their increased output pushes their budget constraint line, *AB,* outward from the origin. As in the classic trade-off of income for leisure, workers are then able to substitute safety for income while moving to an overall level of higher workplace satisfaction. In short, the second position would claim that the industry has become productive enough to "afford" a safer place of employment. Workers move to a higher level of satisfaction, which includes a safer workplace and higher hourly income.

The linking of safety to productivity may not be an acceptable position to many participants in the construction field. After all, the OSHA laws were in part a reflection of organized labor's demand for a safe workplace as a worker's right. The notion of a quid pro quo where safety is traded off for productivity could set a dangerous precedent for collective bargaining agreements if such types of relationships are made explicit. There are serious questions as to the ability of market forces to generate the safety procedures mandated in the 1970s. As was the case for the overall economy, the safety legislation was in part a response to inadequate "voluntary efforts on the part of employers and workers" (Burt 1979, p. 440).

However, the explanations for movements in injury rates can run from one extreme to the other. It is as possible to claim that higher rates occur from overtime, which increases during construction booms. Tight labor supplies and a rush to completion can easily lead to fatigue, miscalculation, and injury. It is also possible to present the contrary scenario, showing that higher injury rates are a result of workplace pressures during recessions. The fears associated with unemployment push workers and managers to take risks in a desperate effort to avoid a layoff. Simply put, the practical realities are that the potential for injury exists at all times in all workplaces. The right of a working person to a safe and healthy atmosphere can run headlong into the economic realities of production costs, profits, and job opportunities.

CHAPTER 15

Conclusions

The economic analysis of the construction industry through its historical roots, applicable theoretical paradigms, and current events has un-
covered a number of recurring themes. Derived demand, productivity,
and the social relations of the building industry are issues that provide
a basis on which to draw some conclusions about the present status of
the industry and its future development.

The boom–bust nature of the industry is accepted as a natural aspect
of life in the building trades. The instability this creates among the
labor force and contracting firms is a well-documented fact. The
quickness with which a union hiring hall bench can be cleared and the
modern overbuilding of commercial space in the late 1980s both reflect tendencies in market-based construction that have carried over
since the nineteenth century.

This should not be seen as a failing on the part of industry participants to understand their own environment. No doubt there are some
who enjoy the feast and famine cycles. Short-run building success can
provide builders with immense financial rewards, and many tradespeople may temporarily bask in the income brought by working "seven-
twelves" (seven days at four to five overtime hours).

The important lesson that can be gleaned from these chapters is that
construction demand is a derived demand. Investment in construction
may be the great harbinger of an impending economic expansion, or it
may be in reaction to an existing spurt of economic growth. Either
way, the wider economy must somehow justify the dollars-and-cents
expenditures for concrete, steel, pipe, and wire.

From the perspective of an overview, it should be noted that the
construction industry is an integral part of a fully developed industrial-

ized economy. With this said, it has been part of the intention of this book to understand those tendencies and characteristics that separate construction from the rest of this industrial landscape. From the outset, the discussions have focused on the peculiar role of hand tools and labor-intensive operations. The continued importance of this feature is not the design of some cadre of traditionally minded industry overseers or the entrenched wishes of narrow-minded union officials. The large labor-hour component found in the installation process is related to the long-run pace of the substitution of capital for labor.

In and of itself, this is an issue that constantly receives a fair amount of attention in most industries. From the scanners at the grocery store checkout counter to computerized laser-guided machine tools, significant replacements of human labor by capital equipment have been occurring across a wide range of industries. Yet the advent of the sophisticated machine and equipment age in the construction industry is ensnared in the age-old character of the building process. Custom-made products, which are installed on site by skilled workers, stand somewhat defiantly in the face of an onslaught by high-technology.

This is not like the case of the Luddites, whose nineteenth-century rebellion against their own industrial future fell victim to the powerful forces pushing for mechanized manufacturing (Sale 1995). It is even difficult to determine in a statistical sense the direction of this substitution at the construction job site. Steven Allen (1985, p. 664) described two conflicting measures of the capital–labor ratio in construction for the period from 1968 to 1978 before settling on an index from the American Productivity Center.

Much in the same fashion in which Douglas Dacy (1965) argued intuitively that changes were afoot in the early post–World War II era, it is hard not to notice the speed with which modern buildings are constructed or renovated. As was discussed in chapter 3, the biggest improvements have been found in the on-site heavy construction sector. What, then, will be the role of the hand tool portion of the job, which remains so clearly connected to physical skills and abilities?

The response has not been one of substituting capital for labor at the immediate point of production. No mechanized finishing carpenter is installing delicate wood paneling or completing an intricate molding design as the final touch to a home renovation. Increasingly, the solution is prefabrication and changes in building products. Off-site production continues as source of cost savings. A lighting fixture manufactured of lightweight materials with fluorescent bulbs installed and electrical connections partially completed can be dropped into a compatible ceiling grid with a minimal amount of effort. Prefabricated tile wall sections can reduce the skilled labor time for a custom-made ceramic tile installation or renovation.

The forces that produce the need to reduce labor hours ultimately have an impact on employment opportunities. An industry that employs over 5 million people necessarily plays a critical role in the economic well-being of this nation. The contradictory nature of casual employment, market uncertainties, and defined building schedules serves to add to the uncertainty of the construction economy. For many industries, market structure adds a degree of stability. The automobile industry has its nucleus of major producers, and consumers are well acquainted with the mainstays of output in the home products markets. For the past 150 years in construction, this has just not been the case.

Proprietorships and partnerships continue to abound in the industry. Low start-up costs, minimal licensing and bonding, the relative ease of access, and mobility across markets have all worked to inhibit economies of scale. The 1977 census of construction industries reported that 18 percent of all firms, or approximately 216,000 companies, were responsible for 76 percent of the total construction business receipts in the survey year. Fifteen years later, the same census found that slightly more than 214,000 shops were accounting for 80 percent of the business generated from the building industry. Despite the experiences of EMCOR and the mergers in the design and engineering segment, consolidation has remained rather consistent.

Although this would seem not to bode well for technical innovation, there is still a driving force that will push technological development. If you have watched laborers pushing a wheelbarrow and dumping their load, or hoisting material by rope and pulley, it is easy to get the feeling that construction is akin to medieval agriculture. With 2 million firms, labor-intensive procedures, and little in the way of industrywide research and development, there are all the makings for barriers to progress. Yet as a derived demand, construction services must meet the needs of increasingly complex high-technology end users and a rapidly evolving technoeconomy. The juxtaposition of the world's most sophisticated computer chip plants being custom built by an industry steeped in traditional practices is inescapable.

Still, it is the construction of these ultra-modern structures with sophisticated building systems and equipment that is moving construction forward. Computerization as such has not taken hold in the field for many specialty contractors, but the general contractor's field office finds computerized job tracking commonplace. After all, if the Sony Walkman and the cellular phone have become work-condition issues (e.g., because of safety or lost-time complaints), it is hard to imagine contractors not improving their production schedules with the newest electronic innovations.

The spillover effect has also influenced the sets of skill requirements. Quinn Mills (1996) presents the interesting view that modern innovations such as telecommuting have to some extent decreased the need for office space. He suggests that builders will need to address the high-tech needs of the next generation of office personnel. From fiber-optic wiring to integrated building service systems to cogeneration plants, there has been growing complexity as well as a simultaneous effort to reduce the hands-on involvement of skilled tradespeople. The electronics revolution has fomented change in construction training at all levels. While the media from time to time report shortages of skilled labor in certain geographic regions, the notion of skill is itself being redefined.

Given the nonstatic but not quite dynamic picture that this text has painted, what can be said for industry productivity? Construction's upward national swing from 1950 through 1968 and its steady decline into the 1980s have ample academic support. The verification of this trend in chapter 9 and the appearance of blocks of years of positive and negative movement (1982–86 is positive; 1987–90 is negative) suggest that the industry still remains at the threshold of change. Hand tools with microchips for accuracy and maintenance functions are already commonplace. Computerized benders such as the Greenlee Company's Smart conduit bender can greatly improve accuracy and efficiency in the electrical trades. The contractor's office is itself being reorganized with computer bidding applications, job management programs, and the electronic ordering of material. Computer-assisted design (CAD) packages continue to fall in price and expand in use. Ipso facto, the long-run growth in real output per construction worker hour found in Figure 9.1 should have had a much steadier upward drift.

The long-run coincidental decline of the building trades unions is certainly an important aspect of the productivity puzzle. Investigators of the productivity issue have focused on union strength and the falling percentage organized as possible sources. Yet productivity gains across the service and manufacturing sectors are not so clearly linked with unionization. The question reverts to the element of skill that is so inexorably woven into the building process.

The many arguments presented in this text point toward a de-skilling process that has been imposed on the industry's workers by external factors. This has adversely impacted both union and nonunion journeypersons who have become proficient in their respective trades. While one set of installation standards is lowered, the industry generates new products with complex designs and operation requirements. Internally, sheet metal workers may find that shop fabrication and lightweight material have decreased their on-site labor time, but that the testing and balancing for building air-handling units have increased in their technical features. The external root of the productivity decline falls into the area of changes in output mix and location of installations. De-skilling occurs as developers and builders move away from high-skilled and, likewise, higher-waged areas.

The declining union market share is in part explained by the fall in demand for construction in union areas. In the absence of hard data, it is still possible to offer some judgments from the preceding chapters as to the direction of union construction. History has shown that American trade unions have great resiliency (the Coopers International remained viable until its merger with the Glass, Molders, and Pottery International in 1992). With estimates as high as 40 percent and as low as 18 percent organized, the building trades have suffered a significant drop in market and political power.

Yet there are signs of revival. Bottom-up organizing through salting campaigns, job targeting, and a variety of project agreement plans have restored some of the verve to the trade union movement. While the unions rarely discuss the repeal of Section 14(b) (right-to-work) or the removal of Section 8(b)(4)(b), which prohibits common situs strike picketing, they have maintained a strong political presence. Davis–Bacon is not a secure piece of legislation, but the basic concepts remain intact. OSHA has survived considerable rounds of debate, and the unions have had their share of judicial victories.

As an economic institution, organized labor must be prepared to serve a collaborative role in the production process. The framework of laws and relations is, in the end, geared toward flexibility and stability. The evidence in the preceding chapters does not make a strong case for union intransigence. Unions have little to gain from adherence to narrow definitions and interpretations. The recognition of the bargaining experience as a collective process is the cornerstone of labor relations in the building industry. Trade unions might consider capitalizing on the give-and-take format of the bargaining process. The growing use of project agreements is an example of this collective adaptability.

From Allan Mandelstamm (1965) to Steven Allen (1986), there has been little evidence of detrimental union action in curtailing productivity. Herbert Northrup (1993) claims that unions have placed themselves at an economic wage disadvantage, and his charges of union interference primarily blame organizing efforts. *NLRB v. Town & Country, Inc.* (1995) was based on the finding that a union member, even one who was a paid organizer, could function as a useful employee during the stipulated workday.

Unions and unionized employers also play a crucial role in skill development. A recurring theme in this analysis has been the mutual benefits to both parties of increased productivity. Formalized training beyond on-the-job instruction has measurable returns for employers and workers. An advantage to the institutional setting of the union sector is that it provides a structured process for developing skilled workers. By establishing standards and upward mobility in apprentice programs, union environments can attract a steady supply of new recruits. Through defined benefit packages and employment plans, unions and their employers break down the resistance of experienced workers to the imparting of knowledge to new entrants.

The Associated Builders and Contractors have concurred with the need for improved training programs, and have established a National Center for Construction Education and Research. The use of pooled resources and certifications for member firms' employees mimics the national joint apprentice training courses found in the union sector. In a survey of nonunion employers in the Erie, New York, building market, Howard Foster (1973) noted that training was consistently a critical concern. Conceptually, training underscores the adage "the future is now." The two major reports presented at the 1991 Construction Industry Institute's annual meeting "urged development of adequate pools of skilled workers" for firms competing in the twenty-first century (Bureau of National Affairs, September 9, 1991, p. 777).

The coming millennium will usher in more than just a host of new techniques and the requisite training. A changing work force composition and a need for new entrants to replace older workers will continue to raise issues about minority and female labor force participation. The ideal result of policies of inclusion will someday be the dropping of the moniker "nontraditional" because it no longer applies. Mixed reviews of past recruitment efforts and the historical record of discrimination ensure that affirmative action and set-aside programs will stay on as significant issues.

That is not to say that the industry has not advanced in creating opportunities for minority and female workers. The statistics reported in chapter 4 point toward increasing participation for minority males, while the trend for females is less obvious. If the assumption is made that barriers such as glass ceilings or discrimination in job assignments still exist in spite of affirmative action, then minority entrants are relegated to a career of slow upward mobility. *Adarand Constructors, Inc., v. Peña* (1995) requires scrutiny before certain types of set-asides for minorities are implemented, while the notion of affirmative action hiring is the object of continuing legal challenges.

Over the past century the construction markets have been strongly influenced by institutions and institutional policies. The nineteenth-century unions did not fall from the sky, but were created by what workers perceived as intolerable conditions of employment. In the 1930s, the Keynesian legislative programs brought order to labor markets that could not find their own common ground. In terms of female and minority employment, it is the union sector that bears much of the brunt of employment demands. The pay differential, fringe benefits, and work environment are the basic reasons for this, although the concept of union representation cannot be dismissed as an additional benefit.

It is in the institutional character of the building trades unions and their collective relations with their employers that the mechanisms exist for improving minority/female labor force participation. The organization, social history, and in-depth training programs are vehicles to upward mobility. Nontraditional workers in the open market find themselves in situations not unlike that of the early construction unionists. Without a collective voice or representation, there is a vacuum that leaves only the government to guarantee equal opportunity.

The government has not shirked that responsibility, but its framework of affirmative action and set-asides has created a considerable debate within the industry. To some extent, these forms of legislation serve to increase friction among both workers and employers. Construction groups' political fortunes wax and wane with the November elections. Yet it is in the realm of public policy that industry participants may find some new directions.

Construction establishments and construction unions have interacted with government on a variety of levels. Chapter 7 outlined the wide reach of the state and the duality of its involvement. The double interest as both an administrator and a purchaser gives government an extraordinary ability to influence the shape and direction of the industry. This is hardly the time to enter the debate about government, but it is evident that economic policies concerning growth and investment have a direct effect on construction activity.

The underpinning of growth is investment, and investment for the construction industry has a very openended list of possibilities. Despite the potential demand for construction services, only a money-backed (effective) demand will do the trick. While investment, growth, and employment in many sectors of the economy experience sustained periods of prosperity, construction continues through its cyclical paces. The problems of unfettered building construction in the midst of a boom period were discussed in chapter 6. The knowledge that, historically, booms and busts move rapidly through a market is incentive enough for employers, developers, and workers to rush to the bandwagon. Propelled by end users' own requirements, it is ludicrous to stand in the way of an investment freight train and say, "Don't build!"

In many respects, government has become the gatekeeper of investment. Fiscal and monetary policy are combined with the public's stake in the administration of the law. Any hint of state planning is in general anathema to the business community. Is it possible to balance the needs of private enterprise with the needs of the general public, yielding employment, income, and increasing standards of living? For a good portion of the post–World War II era, this is exactly what the construction industry was capable of doing. It created millions of decent-paying jobs while employers were able to profit from their investments.

This was not accomplished through a purified free market experiment, but under what can be loosely described as a mixed economy. It is also unfair to argue through rose-colored glasses that the era was without friction, but my focus is on the future. Planning has always been an integral aspect of the building industry. The forms are varied and can range from city planning to corporate capital projects administration. The immense swings in construction investment and employment are in part a result of the lack of commonality in private and public goals. After all, business needs flexibility to respond to market conditions, and public policy is a function of the political process.

In a modern world of high-tech design and brilliant engineering, there is hardly a place for a pattern of declining standards of living. Planning programs that can consider the needs of firms, contractors, government, and construction workers would be able to shield participants from some of the harshness inherent in the periodic surges and shortages in building investment. There is, in such a proposal, a role for the building trades unions. Many have their will expressed through councils or associations, as do many of the employers. It is the role of this collective voice, as described by Richard Freeman and James Medoff (1984), that has been one of the positive accomplishments of the trade union. Policy review could look at employment prospects in the same fashion that it examines a project's long-term impact on local services, tax revenues, or interest rates.

In the final analysis, expansion and growth will be largely dependent on innovation and productivity. Real-wage increases, safer environments, and capital investment have a common market thread. Each must be covered through the value of the job's output. These sources of growth can create enormous opportunities for those presently in the industry and those who are struggling to enter. To create a stable atmosphere in which expansion and economic activity can flourish is the real challenge for unions, workers, employers, and public officials.

BIBLIOGRAPHY

Allen, Steven G. 1983. "Much Ado about Davis–Bacon: A Critical Review and New Evidence." *Journal of Law and Economics*, vol. 26, no. 3 (October): pp. 707–36.
———. 1985. "Why Construction Industry Productivity Is Declining." *Review of Economics and Statistics,* vol. 67, no. 4: pp. 661–69.
———. 1986. "Unionization and Productivity in Office Building and School Construction." *Industrial and Labor Relations Review,* vol. 39, no. 2 (January): pp. 187–201.
———. 1994. "Developments in Collective Bargaining in Construction in the 1980s and 1990s." In *Contemporary Collective Bargaining in the Private Sector,* ed. Paula Voos. Madison, WI: Industrial Relations Research Association, pp. 411–45.
Arno, Peter S. 1984. "The Political Economy of Industrial Injuries." Unpublished Ph.D. dissertation. Graduate Faculty of the New School for Social Research.
Becker, Gary. 1983 [1975]. *Human Capital.* Chicago, Illinois: The University of Chicago Press.
Boorstin, Daniel J. 1965. *The Americans.* New York, NY: Vintage Books.
Borjas, George J. 1979. "Job Satisfaction, Wages and Unions." *Journal of Human Resources,* vol. 14, no. 1 (Winter): pp. 21–40.
Bourdon, Clinton C., and Raymond E. Levitt. 1980. *Union and Open Shop Construction.* Lexington, MA: Lexington Books.
Bowles, Samuel. 1981. "Competitive Wage Determination and Involuntary Unemployment: A Conflict Model." University of Massachusetts at Amherst, Department of Economics.
Bowles, Samuel, David M. Gordon, and Thomas E. Weisskopf. 1983. *Beyond the Waste Land, A Democratic Alternative to Economic Decline.* Garden City, NY: Anchor Press.
Boyer, Richard O., and Herbert M. Morais. 1982. *Labor's Untold Story.* New York: United Electrical, Radio & Machine Workers of America.
Braverman, Harry. 1974. *Labor and Monopoly Capital.* New York: Monthly Review Press.
Bureau of National Affairs. Various 1990–96. *Construction Labor Report.* Washington, DC: Bureau of National Affairs.
Burt, Everett J. 1979. *Labor in the American Economy.* New York: St. Martin's Press.
Carlton, Jim. 1993. "Some Home Builders Find Loans Are Easier to Get as the Market Recovers." *Wall Street Journal,* June 23, A2:3, A6:1
Carlton, Jim, and Mitchell Pacelle. 1992. "Weak Home Market Confers Advantage on Largest Builders." *Wall Street Journal,* January 27, A1:1, A5:3.
Cassimatis, Peter J. 1969. *Economics of the Construction Industry, Studies in Business Economics No. 111.* Washington, DC: The National Industrial Conference Board.

Chandler, Alfred D., Jr. 1965. "The Beginnings of 'Big Business' in American Industry." In *The Shaping of Twentieth-Century America,* ed. Richard M. Abrams and Lawrence W. Levine. Boston, MA: Little, Brown, pp. 62–92.

Coase, Ronald H. 1937. "The Nature of the Firm." *Economica* (November): pp. 386–405.

Commons, John R., David J. Saposs, Helen L. Sumner, E.B. Mittelman, H.E. Hoagland, John B. Andrews, and Selig Perlman. 1936 [1919]. *History of Labor in the United States.* Vols. 1 and 2. New York: Macmillan.

Construction Industry Census Reports. 1967, 1972, 1977, 1982, 1987, 1992. Washington, DC: U.S. Department of Commerce.

Crain's New York Business. 1996. Vol. 12, no. 27.

Cremeans, John E. 1981. "Productivity in the Construction Industry." *Construction Review* (May–June): pp. 4–6.

Dacy, Douglas C. 1965. "Productivity and Price Trends in Construction since 1947." *Review of Economics and Statistics* (November): pp. 406–11.

Dernburg, Thomas F., and Duncan M. MacDougall. 1976. *Macroeconomics: The Measurement, Analysis, and Control of Aggregate Economic Activity.* New York: McGraw-Hill.

Edwards, Richard. 1979. *Contested Terrain.* New York: Basic Books.

Engineering News-Record. 1990–96. New York: McGraw-Hill.

Feldacker, Bruce. 1980. *Labor Guide to Labor Law.* Englewood Cliffs, NJ: Prentice-Hall.

———. 1990. *Labor Guide to Labor Law.* 3d ed. Englewood Cliffs, NJ: Prentice-Hall.

Finkel, Gerald. 1990. "The Determination of Wages for Unionized Construction Electricians in New York City, 1953–1983." Unpublished Ph.D. dissertation. Graduate Faculty of the New School for Social Research.

Fitchen, John. 1986. *Building Construction Before Mechanization.* Cambridge, MA: MIT Press.

Foster, Howard G. 1973. "The Labor Market in Non-Union Construction." *Industrial and Labor Relations Review* (July): pp. 1071–85.

Freeman, Richard B., and James L. Medoff. 1984. *What Do Unions Do?* New York: Basic Books.

Gifford, C.D., ed. 1996. *Directory of U.S. Labor Organizations.* Washington, DC: BNA Books.

Gilpin, Kenneth N. 1993. "JWP's Bankruptcy Plan Will Put the Creditors in Control." *New York Times,* October 12, p. D5.

Gordon, David M. 1974. *Theories of Poverty and Underemployment.* Lexington, MA: DC Heath.

———. 1980. "The Best Defense Is a Good Defense: Towards a Marxian Theory of Labor Union Structure and Behavior." In *New Directions in Labor Economics,* ed. Michael Carter and William Leahy. South Bend, IN: University of Notre Dame Press.

———. 1981. "Capital–Labor Conflict and the Productivity Slowdown." *American Economic Association: Papers and Proceedings.* May.

Gordon, Robert J. 1968. "A New View of Real Investment in Structures, 1919–1966." *Review of Economics and Statistics,* vol. 50, pp. 417–28.

Haber, William, and Harold Levinson. 1956. *Labor Relations in the Building Trades.* Ann Arbor: University of Michigan Press.

Heilbroner, Robert L. 1978. *Beyond Boom and Crash.* New York: W.W. Norton.

Heilbroner, Robert, and Lester Thurow. 1991. *Economics Explained.* Englewood Cliffs, NJ: Touchstone Books.

Hirsch, Barry T., and John T. Addison. 1986. *The Economic Analysis of Unions: New Approaches and Evidence.* Boston: Allen and Unwin.

Hirshleifer, Jack. 1976. *Price Theory and Applications.* Englewood Cliffs, NJ: Prentice Hall.

Hofstader, Richard, William Miller, and Daniel Aaron. 1964. *The Structure of American History.* Englewood Cliffs, NJ: Prentice-Hall.

Kagan, Stephen. 1992. "New York's Vanishing Supply Side." *City Journal* (Autumn): pp. 33–40.

Kahn, Lawrence M. 1978. "The Effects of Unions on the Earnings of Non-union Workers." *Industrial and Labor Relations Review,* vol. 31, no. 2 (January): pp. 205–16.

Keynes, John Maynard. 1964 [1936]. *The General Theory of Employment, Interest, and Money.* New York: Harbinger Books.

"Labor Letter: A Special News Report on People and Their Jobs in Offices, Fields and Factories." 1993. *Wall Street Journal,* February 22, A1:5.

Lewis, H. Gregg. 1963. *Unionism and Relative Wages in the U.S.: An Empirical Inquiry.* Chicago: University of Chicago Press.

———. 1986. *Union Relative Wage Effects: A Survey.* Chicago: University of Chicago Press.

McCaffree, Kenneth M. 1955–56. "Regional Labor Agreements in the Construction Industry." *Industrial and Labor Relations Review,* vol. 9, pp. 594–609.

McElvaine, Robert S. 1984. *The Great Depression.* New York: Times Books.

Mandelstamm, Allan B. 1965. "The Effects of Unions on Efficiency in the Residential Construction Industry: A Case Study." *Industrial and Labor Relations Review* (July): pp. 503–21.

Marglin, Stephen A. 1974. "What Do Bosses Do? The Origins and Functions of Hierarchy in Capitalist Production." *Review of Radical Political Economics,* vol. 6, no. 2 (Summer): pp. 33–60.

Marshall, F. Ray, Allan M. Cartter, and Allan G. King. 1976. *Labor Economics, Wages, Employment, and Trade Unionism.* Homewood, IL: Richard D. Irwin.

Marx, Karl. 1974 [1887]. *Capital.* Frederick Engels, ed. Vols. 1–3. Moscow: Progress Publishers.

Mathews, Robert Charles Oliver. 1959. *The Business Cycle.* Chicago: University of Chicago Press.

Mills, Daniel Q. 1972a. "Construction Wage Stabilization: A Historic Perspective." *Industrial Relations* (October): pp. 350–65.

———. 1972b. *Industrial Relations and Manpower in Construction.* Cambridge, MA: MIT Press.

Mills, Quinn. 1996. *Staying Afloat in the Construction Industry.* Washington, DC: BNI Publications.

New York State Employment Review. 1990. Albany, NY: New York State Department of Labor.

New York State Organized Crime Task Force. 1988. *Corruption and Racketeering in the N.Y.C. Construction Industry.* Interim Report. Ithaca, NY: ILR Press.

Northrup, Herbert R. 1993. "Salting the Contractors' Labor Force: Construction Unions Organizing with NLRB Assistance." *Journal of Labor Research,* vol. 14, no. 4 (Fall): pp. 469–92.

Palladino, Grace. 1991. *Dreams of Dignity, Workers of Vision: A History of the International Brotherhood of Electrical Workers.* Washington, DC: International Brotherhood of Electrical Workers.

Palmer, R.R., and Joel Colton. 1965. *A History of the Modern World.* New York: Alfred A. Knopf.

Personick, Martin E. 1974. "Union and Nonunion Pay Patterns in Construction." *Monthly Labor Review* (August): p. 71.

Pfeffer, Jeffrey, and Jerry Ross. 1980. "Union–Non-Union Effects on Wage and Status Attainment." *Industrial Relations* (Spring): pp. 140–51.

Philips, Peter, Garth Mangum, Norm Waitzman, and Anne Yeagle. 1995. *Losing Ground: Lessons from the Repeal of Nine "Little Davis–Bacon" Acts.* Salt Lake City: University of Utah, Department of Economics.

Ruegg, Rosalie T., and Harold E. Marshall. 1990. *Building Economics Theory and Practice.* New York: Van Nostrand Reinhold.

Sale, Kirkpatrick. 1995. *Rebels Against the Future.* Reading, MA: Addison-Wesley.

Schapner, M.B. 1975. *American Labor: A Bicentennial History.* Washington, DC: Public Affairs Press.

Shilling, A. Gary. 1988. *After the Crash.* Short Hills, NJ: Lake View Economic Services.

Sider, Hal. 1983. "Safety and Productivity in Underground Coal Mining." *Review of Economics and Statistics* (May): pp. 225–33.

Smith, Adam. 1977 [1776]. *The Wealth of Nations,* ed. Andrew Skinner. New York: Penguin Books.

Sobotka, Stephen. 1953. "Union Influence on Wages: The Construction Industry." *Journal of Political Economy,* vol. 61 (April): pp. 61–97.

Stone, Katherine. 1974. "The Origins of Job Structures in the Steel Industry." *Review of Radical Political Economics,* vol. 6, no. 2 (Summer): pp. 61–97.

U.S. Department of Commerce. 1978. "Historical Series." *Construction Review* (December). Washington, DC: Government Printing Office.

———. 1989–96. *Construction Review, Quarterly Industry Report.* Washington, DC: Government Printing Office.

———. 1990–95. *Survey of Current Business.* Various issues. Washington, DC: Government Printing Office.

———. Bureau of the Census, 1967, 1972, 1977, 1982, 1987, 1992. *Census of Construction Industries. United States Summary, Establishments with and without Payroll.* Washington, DC: Government Printing Office.

———. 1987. *Economic Census, Survey of Minority-Owned Business Enterprises.* Washington, DC: Government Printing Office.

———. 1987, 1992. *Economic Census, Survey of Women-Owned Business Enterprises.* Washington, DC: Government Printing Office.

————. 1990–93. *County Business Patterns.* Washington, DC: Government Printing Office.

U.S. Department of Labor. 1975. *Code of Federal Regulations* (CFR). Part 1926. Washington, DC: Government Printing Office.

————. Bureau of Labor Statistics. 1996. "Union Members in 1995." *Household Data Survey* (February 9). Washington, DC: Government Printing Office.

Vincent, Jeff. 1990. "Indiana's Prevailing Wage Law: A Preliminary Evaluation of Its Impact on the State Construction Industry." *Labor Studies Journal,* vol. 15, no. 3 (Fall): pp. 17–31.

INDEX

Gerald Finkel was born in Jersey City and is a second-generation Local No. 3 International Brotherhood of Electrical Workers journey-person. After receiving a B.A from Rutgers College, he became an electrician's apprentice. While working in the field as a journeyman, foreman, shop steward, and assistant project manager, Gerald earned a master's in political economy and a Ph.D. in labor economics from the Graduate Faculty of the New School for Social Research at night. At present, he is director of the Educational and Cultural Trust Fund of the Joint Industry Board of the Electrical Industry. He is also an adjunct professor of economics at the Harry Van Arsdale Jr. School for Labor Studies at SUNY Empire State College, and is an occasional instructor in the Cornell–ILR Trade Union Program. His major research papers include "Determination of Wages for New York City Unionized Construction Electricians" and "The Span of Control in the Telephone Industry." Gerald lives in New York City with his wife, Helen, and their daughters, Margot and Suzanne.